D1325829

·TESCO· COOKERY· COLLECTION·
CHEESECAKES

TESCO

Published exclusively for Tesco Stores Ltd,
Delamare Road, Cheshunt, Herts. EN8 9SL
by Cathay Books, 59 Grosvenor Street, London W1

First published 1985
Reprinted 1985

© Cathay Books 1985
ISBN 0 86178 299 2

Printed in Hong Kong

ACKNOWLEDGEMENTS

The publishers would like to thank the following companies
for their kindness in providing materials and equipment
used in the photography for this book.
David Mellor, 4 Sloane Square, London SW1
Elizabeth David, 46 Bourne Street, London SW1
World's End Tiles, British Rail Yard, Silverthorne Road, London SW8

We would also like to thank the following who
were concerned in the preparation of the book.

Series Art Director Pedro Prá-Lopez
Editor Stella Henvey
Photographer Martin Brigdale with *stylist* Liz Allen-Eslor
Food prepared for photography by Jacki Baxter

CONTENTS

NOTE

Standard spoon measurements are used in all recipes

1 tablespoon (tbls) = one 15 ml spoon
1 teaspoon (tsp) = one 5 ml spoon
All spoon measures are level

All eggs are sizes 3 or 4 (standard) unless otherwise stated.

For all recipes, quantities are given in both
metric and imperial measures. Follow either set
but not a mixture of both, as they are not interchangeable.

We set up our Consumer Advisory Service in response to the many pleas for information and cooking ideas we received from our customers. It is run by our team of qualified home economists who answer queries, offer practical advice on cookery and the home and give talks and demonstrations on new products and equipment.

The resounding success of the service and the continued demand for more and more recipes and information has now prompted us to produce our own special range of Tesco Cookery Books.

Our series starts with 12 books, each one focusing on an area that our customers have shown particular interest in. Each book contains practical background information on the chosen subject and concentrates on a wide selection of carefully tested recipes, each one illustrated in colour.

Cheesecakes for instance shows you step-by-step, how to line your baking tins and prepare the other ingredients before embarking on a whole selection of superb, and unusual recipes. From simple no-cook cheesecakes and spectacular desserts to some fabulous savoury cheesecakes which are perfect for buffets and dinner parties, this special Tesco collection will guarantee you reliable and delicious results.

I very much hope you will enjoy looking through the pages which follow, trying out the recipes and above all tasting and enjoying the results. Happy Cooking!

Carey Dennis, senior home economist, Tesco Stores Ltd.

INTRODUCTION

Cheesecakes are sinfully rich, wickedly tempting – and totally irresistible! Many countries have their own favourite recipes, which can vary from a simple flan type to an elaborate, gâteau-like confection.

There are two basic kinds of cheesecake: those that are baked and those that are uncooked and chilled. Either type can be sweet or savoury. Dessert cheesecakes are most familiar, and ideal for parties as they look stunning and can be prepared well in advance. Savoury cheesecakes are equally glamorous – perfect buffet food – and make an exciting addition to your cooking repertoire.

Baked cheesecakes are essentially rich, moist and creamy, with a thick 'close' texture. To prevent the filling separating, a small quantity of flour, semolina or ground nuts such as almonds or hazelnuts, is usually included and the cheesecake is baked in a moderate oven. When set, the filling should be soft but spongy and a skewer or sharp, narrow knife inserted into the centre should come out clean. (If the mixture flows freely together again, the filling is not yet set.)

Uncooked chilled cheesecakes: the simplest type is made by spreading a well-flavoured, thick cheese filling in a prepared pastry, sponge or biscuit case and chilling it in the refrigerator until firm. The modern American-style cheesecake has a crunchy biscuit base and uses gelatine to set the filling.

Basic bases

For a biscuit base, crushed biscuits are combined with melted margarine or butter and pressed evenly over the base of the tin. The mixture is then chilled in the refrigerator until firm. (See steps for making a biscuit base and case on p.6.) The biscuits can be sweet, plain or savoury, depending on the filling. Additional ingredients for sweet cheesecake bases include sugar (which can be melted with the fat for extra smoothness, or simply stirred into the crumb mixture), ground spices, grated citrus rind and chopped or ground nuts. Bases for savoury cheesecakes can be flavoured with herbs, seasonings, finely grated hard cheese or nuts.

As an alternative to biscuits you can use crackers, rusks, porridge oats, wheatflakes or, for sweet cheesecakes, muesli or puffed rice.

Pastry is another useful cheesecake base. Shortcrust is suitable for both sweet and savoury fillings. A sweet shortcrust, enriched with egg yolk, is ideal for cheesecakes made with fruit.

For uncooked cheesecakes the pastry is always cooked in advance. In the case of baked cheesecakes the pastry can be baked blind for extra crispness or cooked with the filling. (See steps for making a pastry case on p.6.)

Sponge cake makes an appetizing soft base for a sweet filling. You can use a home-made cake mixture or a commercial sponge layer or flan case.

Choosing the cheese

Fresh soft cheese is the essential ingredient of a cheesecake. A variety of types are suitable, including full fat soft, curd, cottage and skimmed milk cheeses. European fresh soft cheeses – Quark, Ricotta, Fromage blanc and Fromage frais, Demi-sel and Petit Suisse – all give good results.

Take care when choosing full fat soft cheese for a baked cheesecake. Look for a 'stabilized' brand, or a cream cheese with a fat content no higher than 30 per cent. Richer cheeses become grainy if overbeaten and can separate during baking.

Step-by-step basic biscuit base

1 Place the biscuits in a strong polythene bag, squeeze out the air and tie the top. Roll a rolling pin back and forth over the bag, until the biscuits are reduced to crumbs, or reduce the biscuits to crumbs in a food processor.

2 Melt the margarine or butter in a saucepan over low heat. Remove from the heat, tip in the biscuit crumbs and stir vigorously with a wooden spoon until evenly combined.

3 Spoon the crumb mixture into the greased tin. Using the back of the spoon, press the mixture firmly and evenly over the base of the tin.

Step-by-step biscuit case

1 Lightly grease a loose-bottomed metal flan tin with plain sides. Line base with biscuit crumbs as in text above.

2 Tilt the tin towards you, spoon some of the mixture on to the area nearest you. Press down with the back of the spoon.

3 Continue until the sides are evenly coated. Roll a straight-sided jar over the base and around the sides to finish.

Step-by-step pastry case

1 Use some of the pastry to line the base of the tin only. Chill, or bake and cool according to the recipe.

2 Measure the depth and diameter of the tin with string. Roll out the remaining pastry to a rectangle, slightly longer than the diameter and twice as wide as the depth. Cut lengthways.

3 Replace the sides of the tin on the base. Place each pastry strip around the sides of the tin, pressing the bottom edge on to the pastry base and sealing the joins firmly. Neaten the top edge.

6

Continental cheesecake

SERVES 8

For the base
100g (4oz) plain flour
pinch of salt
50g (2oz) margarine or butter, diced
15g (½oz) caster sugar
1 tbls cold water
For the filling
75g (3oz) butter
75g (3oz) caster sugar
2 eggs, lightly beaten
225g (8oz) curd cheese, softened
grated rind of 1 lemon
2 tbls lemon juice
25g (1oz) ground almonds

Grease a 23cm (9 inch) flan ring on a baking sheet.

Sift the flour with the salt into a mixing bowl. Add the margarine and rub it in with the fingertips until the mixture resembles fine breadcrumbs. Stir in the sugar. Sprinkle over the water and draw the mixture together to make a firm dough, adding a little more cold water if necessary, to bind.

Turn the dough on to a lightly floured surface and knead gently for 1 minute, until smooth. Roll out on a lightly floured surface and use to line the greased flan ring. Do not trim. Chill in the refrigerator for 20 minutes to allow the pastry to relax, then trim. Meanwhile, heat the oven to 180°C, 350°F, Gas Mark 4.

To make the filling, cream the butter and sugar together in a bowl until light and fluffy, then gradually beat in the eggs, alternating with the cheese. When thoroughly blended, stir in the lemon rind and juice and the ground almonds, mixing well.

Pour the filling into the prepared flan ring and bake in the oven for 45 minutes, or until set.

Leave the cheesecake for 3-4 hours, until cold, then remove from the ring and transfer to a serving plate.

Variation: Scatter 25g (1oz) seedless raisins over the base of the pastry case before pouring in the filling.

American cheesecake

SERVES 10-12

For the base
75g (3oz) margarine or butter, melted
175g (6oz) digestive biscuits, crushed
For the filling
1 kg (2 lb) full fat soft cheese
250g (9oz) caster sugar
4 eggs, lightly beaten
40g (1½oz) plain flour, sifted
284 ml (10 fl oz) carton soured cream
grated rind of 1 lemon
fresh or drained canned cherries, to
  decorate

Heat the oven to 180°C, 350°F, Gas Mark 4.

Grease a loose-bottomed or springform 23cm (9 inch) cake tin. Mix the melted margarine with the biscuit crumbs. Spoon into the greased tin and press evenly over the base. Place on a baking sheet and bake in the oven for 10 minutes, then set aside to cool.

Beat together all the ingredients for the filling except the cherries and pour into the tin on the baking sheet. Bake in the oven for 35 minutes, or until set. Leave for 3-4 hours, until cold.

Run a round-bladed knife around the sides of the cheesecake, then remove from the tin. Transfer to a serving plate and decorate with cherries.

Honey nut cheesecake

SERVES 8

For the base
50 g (2 oz) margarine or butter, melted
3 tbls golden syrup, warmed
175 g (6 oz) porridge oats
1 egg yolk
For the filling
225 g (8 oz) full fat soft cheese
3 eggs, separated
4 tbls thick honey
25 g (1 oz) plain flour, sifted
4 tbls double or whipping cream
*100 g (4 oz) walnuts, coarsely
    chopped*
50 g (2 oz) caster sugar
For the topping
3 tbls thick honey
*100 g (4 oz) walnuts, coarsely
    chopped*

Heat the oven to 160°C, 325°F, Gas Mark 3. Grease a loose-bottomed or spring-form 18-20 cm (7-8 inch) tin.

Mix the margarine with the syrup, oats and egg yolk. Spoon into the greased tin and press evenly over the base. Chill in the refrigerator while making the filling.

Beat the cheese in a bowl until softened. Beat in the egg yolks, honey, flour, cream and chopped walnuts. Whisk the egg whites until stiff, then whisk in the caster sugar. Using a large metal spoon, fold lightly, but thoroughly, into the cheese mixture. Turn the mixture into the prepared tin and smooth the surface.

Place the cheesecake on a baking sheet and bake in the oven for 1½-1¾ hours or until the filling is set. Leave the cheesecake to cool for 1 hour.

To make the topping, melt the honey in a saucepan over low heat. Remove from the heat and stir in the chopped walnuts, then spoon over the top of the cheesecake. Leave the cheesecake for a further 2-3 hours, until cold. Chill in the refrigerator for 2-3 hours.

Run a round-bladed knife around the sides of the cheesecake, remove from the tin and transfer to a plate.

● Top left: Honey nut cheesecake

8

● Top: American cheesecake (page 7); Continental cheesecake (page 7)

Squashy rhubarb cheesecake

SERVES 8

For the base
75 g (3 oz) margarine or butter, melted
50 g (2 oz) caster sugar
grated rind of 1 orange
good pinch of ground ginger
175 g (6 oz) digestive biscuits, crushed
For the filling
225 g (8 oz) fresh rhubarb, chopped
4 tbls fresh orange juice
175 g (6 oz) caster sugar
227 g (8 oz) carton curd or sieved
*   cottage cheese*
3 eggs, separated
25 g (1 oz) plain flour
¼ tsp ground ginger
For the topping
75 g (3 oz) plain flour
40 g (1½ oz) margarine or butter,
*   diced*
50 g (2 oz) demerara sugar
142 ml (5 fl oz) carton double cream, to
*   decorate*
coloured sugar crystals (optional)

Grease a loose-bottomed or spring-form 18-20 cm (7-8 inch) cake tin.

Mix the melted margarine with the sugar, orange rind, ginger and biscuit crumbs. Spoon into the greased tin and press evenly over the base. Chill the biscuit base in the refrigerator while making the rhubarb filling.

Put the rhubarb into a non-stick saucepan with the orange juice and 50 g (2 oz) of the caster sugar. Cover and cook gently for about 10-15 minutes, or until tender. Remove from the heat and leave to cool.

Meanwhile, heat the oven to 160°C, 325°F, Gas Mark 3.

Beat the cheese in a bowl until softened. Beat in the egg yolks, half the remaining caster sugar and the rhubarb. Sift in the flour and ginger and beat well until thoroughly blended.

Whisk the egg whites until stiff, then whisk in the remaining caster sugar. Using a large metal spoon, fold lightly, but thoroughly, into the cheese and rhubarb mixture. Turn into the prepared tin and smooth the surface.

To make the topping, sift the flour into a mixing bowl. Add the margarine and rub it in with the fingertips until the mixture resembles coarse breadcrumbs. Stir in the sugar. Sprinkle evenly over the top of the cheesecake.

Place the cheesecake on a baking sheet and bake in the oven for 1½-1¾ hours, or until the filling is set.

Remove the cheesecake from the oven and leave to cool for 1 hour. Run a round-bladed knife around the sides, then remove from the tin. Transfer the cheesecake to a serving plate.

Whip the cream until soft peaks form. Spread the cream around the sides of the cheesecake. Sprinkle the cream with sugar crystals, if liked. Chill for at least 2 hours before serving.

Variation: For Squashy plum cheesecake, use stoned plums in place of rhubarb.

Pineapple wholefood cheesecake

SERVES 6

For the base
75 g (3 oz) margarine or butter, melted
1 tsp ground cinnamon
1 tsp soft dark brown sugar
175 g (6 oz) wholemeal bran biscuits,
*   crushed*
For the filling
227 g (8 oz) carton curd cheese
3 tbls clear honey
142 ml (5 fl oz) carton soured cream
1 egg yolk
1 small ripe fresh pineapple, peeled,
*   cored and chopped*
1-2 tbls sesame seeds

Heat the oven to 180°C, 350°F, Gas Mark 4. Grease a loose-bottomed or spring-form 20-23 cm (8-9 inch) cake tin.

Mix the melted margarine with the cinnamon, sugar and biscuit crumbs.

Spoon into the greased tin and press evenly over the base. Chill in the refrigerator while making the filling.

Put the cheese, honey, soured cream and egg yolk into a bowl and beat together until evenly blended. Pour the mixture into the tin. Place the cheesecake on a baking sheet. Bake in the oven for 30 minutes, or until just set. Leave the cheesecake for 3-4 hours, until cold.

Remove the cheesecake from the tin and transfer to a serving plate. Arrange the pineapple in a ring around the top of the cheesecake. Sprinkle the sesame seeds in the centre.

Serving ideas: Serve this cheesecake with thick natural yoghurt or lightly whipped double or whipping cream.
Variations: Other fresh fruit, such as hulled strawberries, raspberries, sliced kiwi fruit, melon cubes or balls or halved and seeded grapes, can be used instead of pineapple.

For extra interest, decorate the cheesecake with sprigs of mint or lemon balm.

• Squashy rhubarb cheesecake; Pineapple wholefood cheesecake

Mocha cheesecake

SERVES 8

For the base
75 g (3 oz) plain flour
50 g (2 oz) icing sugar
50 g (2 oz) margarine or butter, diced
50 g (2 oz) hazelnuts, finely chopped
1 egg yolk
1 tbls double cream
For the filling
1½ tsp instant coffee powder
1½ tsp drinking chocolate powder
2 tbls boiling water
227 g (8 oz) carton curd or sieved
    cottage cheese
3 eggs, separated
50 g (2 oz) soft light brown sugar
25 g (1 oz) plain flour, sifted
150 g (5.29 oz) carton hazelnut or
    muesli yoghurt
50 g (2 oz) caster sugar
For the topping
½ tsp instant coffee powder
½ tsp drinking chocolate powder
2 tsp boiling water
142 (5 fl oz) carton soured cream
50 g (2 oz) coffee beans or toasted
    skinned hazelnuts, to decorate

Heat the oven to 160°C, 325°F, Gas Mark 3. Grease a loose-bottomed or spring-form 18-20 cm (7-8 inch) cake tin.

Sift the flour with the icing sugar into a mixing bowl. Add the margarine and rub it in with the fingertips until the mixture resembles fine breadcrumbs. Stir in the hazelnuts. Beat the egg yolk with the cream and stir into the rubbed-in mixture. Draw the mixture together to make a soft dough.

Shape into a ball and press evenly over the base of the greased tin. Chill in refrigerator while making filling.

Dissolve the instant coffee and drinking chocolate in the boiling water and set aside. Beat the cheese in a bowl until softened. Beat in the egg yolks, brown sugar, flour, yoghurt and the coffee and chocolate liquid.

Whisk the egg whites until stiff, then whisk in the caster sugar. Using a large metal spoon, fold lightly, but thoroughly, into the cheese mixture. Turn into the tin and smooth the surface.

Bake in the oven for 1½-1¾ hours or until the filling is set. Cool for 1 hour.

Run a round-bladed knife around the sides of the cheesecake, then remove from the tin. Transfer the cheesecake to a serving plate.

To make the topping, dissolve the coffee and drinking chocolate in the boiling water. Allow to cool, then stir into the soured cream and spread over the top of the cheesecake. Chill the cheesecake in the refrigerator for at least 2 hours. Decorate with coffee beans or hazelnuts just before serving.

● Bottom: Mocha cheesecake;
Top right: Devil's food cheesecake

Devil's food cheesecake

SERVES 8

For the base
75 g (3 oz) margarine or butter, melted
25 g (1 oz) caster sugar
175 g (6 oz) chocolate digestive
    biscuits, crushed

For the filling
100 g (4 oz) plain dessert chocolate
300 g (10 oz) full fat soft cheese
3 eggs, separated
1 tsp gravy browning
50 g (2 oz) soft dark brown sugar
25 g (1 oz) plain flour, sifted
142 ml (5 fl oz) carton soured cream
50 g (2 oz) caster sugar

For the frosting
225 g (8 oz) sugar
150 ml (¼ pint) water
175 g (6 oz) plain dessert chocolate
50 g (2 oz) margarine or butter

Heat the oven to 160°C, 325°F, Gas Mark 3. Grease a loose-bottomed or spring-form 18-20 cm (7-8 inch) tin.

Mix the melted margarine with the sugar and biscuit crumbs. Spoon into the greased tin and press evenly over the base. Chill while making the filling.

Break the chocolate into pieces and place in a heatproof bowl set over a saucepan of hot water. Heat gently, until melted. Remove from heat.

Beat the cheese in a bowl until softened. Beat in the egg yolks, gravy browning, brown sugar, flour, soured cream and melted chocolate. Whisk the egg whites until stiff, then whisk in the caster sugar. Fold into the cheese mixture. Turn into the prepared tin and smooth the surface.

Place the cheesecake on a baking sheet and bake in the oven for 1½-1¾ hours or until set. Cool for 1 hour.

Run a round-bladed knife around the sides of the cheesecake, then remove from the tin to a wire rack.

To make the frosting, put the sugar and water into a saucepan and stir over low heat until the sugar has dissolved. Bring to the boil and boil gently until syrupy. Remove from the heat and add the chocolate, broken into small pieces. Beat vigorously until melted. Add the margarine and beat until thick and glossy.

Swirl the frosting over the top and sides of the cheesecake. Transfer to a plate and chill for 2-3 hours.

Coconut cheesecake

SERVES 8

For the base
50 g (2 oz) self-raising flour
½ tsp baking powder
25 g (1 oz) desiccated coconut
50 g (2 oz) margarine or butter
50 g (2 oz) caster sugar
1 egg
For the filling
150 ml (¼ pint) milk
75 g (3 oz) desiccated coconut
225 g (8 oz) full fat soft cheese
1 tbls fresh lime juice
3 eggs, separated
100 g (4 oz) caster sugar
25 g (1 oz) plain flour, sifted
For the icing
175 g (6 oz) icing sugar
1-2 tbls lime juice
few drops of green food colouring
To decorate
50 g (2 oz) desiccated coconut, toasted
lime slices

First make the coconut infusion for the filling. Heat the milk to just below boiling point, stir in the coconut and set aside for 30 minutes.

Meanwhile, heat the oven to 160°C, 325°F, Gas Mark 3. Grease a loose-bottomed or spring-form 18-20 cm (7-8 inch) cake tin.

To make the base, sift the flour with the baking powder into a mixing bowl. Add the coconut, margarine, sugar and egg. Beat with a wooden spoon for 2 minutes, or with a hand-held electric whisk for 1 minute, until thoroughly blended. Spread the mixture evenly over the base of the tin.

To make the filling, beat the cheese in a bowl until softened. Beat in the lime juice, egg yolks, half the sugar and the flour. Strain the milk from the coconut, pressing the coconut firmly against the sieve to extract as much flavour as possible. Beat the coconut milk into the cheese mixture.

Whisk the egg whites until stiff, then whisk in the remaining sugar. Using a large metal spoon, fold lightly, but thor-oughly, into the cheese mixture. Turn the mixture into the prepared tin and smooth the surface.

Bake in the oven for 1½-1¾ hours, or until the filling is set. Leave the cheese-cake to cool for 1 hour.

Run a round-bladed knife around the sides of the cheesecake, then re-move from the tin.

To make the icing, sift the icing sugar into a mixing bowl and stir in sufficient lime juice to give a fairly stiff, spreading consistency. Tint pale green with food colouring.

Spread the icing over the top and sides of the cheesecake. Sprinkle with toasted coconut and decorate with lime slices. Transfer the cheesecake to a serving plate and chill for 2-3 hours.

Variation: Use orange juice instead of lime, and yellow food colouring.

Heavenly cheesecake

SERVES 8

For the base
50 g (2 oz) self-raising flour
½ tsp baking powder
50 g (2 oz) margarine or butter, softened
50 g (2 oz) caster sugar
1 egg
a few drops of cochineal
For the filling
300 g (11 oz) full fat soft cheese
40 g (1½ oz) plain flour, sifted
142 ml (5 fl oz) carton whipping cream
a few drops of vanilla essence
5 egg whites
100 g (4 oz) caster sugar
For the icing
225 g (8 oz) icing sugar
1 egg white, lightly whisked
crystallized rose petals to decorate

Heat the oven to 160°C, 325°F, Gas Mark 3. Thoroughly grease a loose-bottomed or spring-form 18-20 cm (7-8 inch) cake tin.

Sift the flour with the baking powder into a mixing bowl. Add the margarine,

14

sugar, egg and cochineal. Beat with a wooden spoon for 2 minutes, or with a hand-held electric whisk for 1 minute, until thoroughly blended. Spread the mixture evenly over the base of the tin.

To make the filling, beat the cheese in a bowl until softened. Beat in the flour, cream, vanilla essence, 1 egg white and half the sugar. Whisk the remaining egg whites until stiff, then whisk in the remaining sugar. Fold lightly, but thoroughly, into the cheese mixture.

Turn the mixture into the prepared tin. Bake in the oven for 1½-1¾ hours, or until set. Cool for 1 hour.

Run a round-bladed knife around the sides of the cheesecake, then remove from the tin. Transfer to a plate.

To make the icing, sift the icing sugar into a mixing bowl and beat in the egg white. Swirl the icing over the cheesecake and leave until just beginning to set, then scatter over the rose petals. Chill for 2-3 hours.

• Top: Coconut cheesecake; Bottom: Heavenly cheesecake

Marbled cheesecake

SERVES 6

For the base
225g (8oz) plain flour
25g (1oz) icing sugar
100g (4oz) margarine or butter,
softened
1 egg yolk
For the filling
25g (1oz) plain dessert chocolate
450g (1 lb) full fat soft cheese
2 tbls plain flour, sifted
200g (7oz) caster sugar
2 eggs
2 egg yolks
2½ tbls double or whipping cream
2 tsp brandy
grated rind of ½ orange

Sift the flour with the icing sugar into a mixing bowl. Add the margarine and egg yolk and work to a soft dough with the fingertips. Shape the dough into a ball, then wrap in foil or cling film and chill in the refrigerator for 20 minutes.

Heat the oven to 200°C, 400°F, Gas Mark 6. Grease a 20cm (8 inch) flan ring on a baking sheet.

Roll out the dough on a lightly floured surface and use to line the greased flan ring. Prick the base all over with a fork and bake in the oven for 15 minutes until golden. Remove from the oven, transfer to a wire rack and leave to cool.

Increase the oven heat to 230°C, 450°F, Gas Mark 8.

To make the filling, break the chocolate into pieces and place in a small heatproof bowl set over a saucepan of hot water. Heat gently, stirring occasionally, until the chocolate has melted. Remove from the heat.

Beat the cheese in a bowl until softened. Beat in the flour, sugar, eggs, egg yolks and cream. Spoon one-third of the cheese mixture into a separate bowl and stir in the melted chocolate and brandy. Stir the orange rind into the cheese mixture in the other bowl.

Pour the orange-flavoured mixture into the prepared pastry case. Place spoonfuls of the chocolate mixture on the top and swirl them through the orange-flavoured mixture with a round-bladed knife, to give a marbled effect. Bake in the oven for 15 minutes. Reduce the oven heat to 110°C, 225°F, Gas Mark ½ and bake for a further 50-65 minutes, or until the chocolate and orange marbled filling is set.

Leave the cheesecake for 3-4 hours, until cold, then chill in the refrigerator overnight. Run a round-bladed knife around the sides of the cheesecake, then remove from the ring. Transfer the cheesecake to a serving plate. Serve chilled.

Variation: Arrange drained canned mandarin oranges or fresh orange slices around the edge of the cheesecake. Serve with grated chocolate.

Cinnamon apple cheesecake

SERVES 8

For the base
225g (8oz) plain flour
175g (6oz) margarine or butter, diced
25g (1oz) icing sugar
1 egg yolk
For the filling
50g (2oz) butter, softened
50g (2oz) sugar
227g (8oz) carton cottage cheese,
sieved
½ × 410g (14½oz) can stewed apple
3 tbls plain flour
2-3 tsp ground cinnamon
4 eggs, separated

Heat the oven to 200°C, 400°F, Gas Mark 6. Grease a 10 × 37cm (4 × 14½ inch) baking tin.

Sift the flour into a bowl. Add the margarine and rub it in with the fingertips until the mixture resembles coarse breadcrumbs. Sift in the icing sugar and stir thoroughly to mix. Beat the egg yolk with a few drops of water, then add to the rubbed-in mixture and mix to a firm dough.

16

● Marbled cheesecake; Cinnamon apple cheesecake

Knead the dough lightly for 1 minute, then roll it out on a lightly floured surface and use to line the base and sides of the greased tin. Trim the edges, reserving the trimming for decoration.

To make the filling, cream the butter and sugar in a bowl until light and fluffy. Stir in the cheese and apple. Sift in the flour and cinnamon, then add the egg yolks and beat well until the mixture is evenly blended.

Whisk the egg whites until stiff. Using a large metal spoon, fold lightly, but thoroughly, into the cheese mixture. Spoon the filling into the prepared

pastry case and smooth the surface.

Roll out the reserved pastry trimmings and cut into strips. Dampen the ends, then arrange the strips in a lattice pattern over the filling. Press the ends of the strips on the edge of the pastry case to seal.

Bake in the oven for 35-40 minutes, or until the pastry is golden and the filling is set.

Serving ideas: This cheesecake is delicious hot or warm as a pudding with pouring cream or scoops of vanilla ice cream, or cold as a cake for tea.

Apricot cheesecake

SERVES 8

For the base
75 g (3 oz) margarine or butter, melted
50 g (2 oz) soft light brown sugar
100 g (4 oz) porridge oats
1 egg yolk
For the filling and decoration
2 × 425 g (15 oz) cans apricot halves,
drained
227 g (8 oz) carton curd cheese
3 eggs, separated
a few drops of almond essence
100 g (4 oz) caster sugar
25 g (1 oz) plain flour, sifted
284 ml (10 fl oz) carton whipping
cream

Heat the oven to 160°C, 325°F, Gas Mark 3. Grease a loose-bottomed or spring-form 18-20 cm (7-8 inch) tin.

Mix the melted margarine with the sugar, oats and egg yolk. Spoon into the greased tin and press evenly over base. Chill in the refrigerator while making the filling.

Reserve 8 apricot halves for decoration. Chop the remaining apricots and scatter over the oat base.

Beat the cheese in a bowl. Beat in the egg yolks, almond essence, half the sugar, the flour and half the cream.

Whisk the egg whites until stiff, then whisk in the remaining sugar. Using a large metal spoon, fold lightly, but thoroughly, into the cheese mixture. Turn into the tin and smooth the surface.

Place the cheesecake on a baking sheet and bake in the oven for 1½-1¾ hours, or until the filling is set. Leave the cheesecake for 3-4 hours, until cold. Run a round-bladed knife around the sides of the cheesecake, then remove from the tin. Transfer to a plate.

Whip the remaining cream until it forms soft peaks. Pipe whirls of cream around the edge of the cheesecake. Slice the reserved apricots lengthways and use to decorate.

Duchess cheesecake

SERVES 8

For the base
75 g (3 oz) margarine or butter, melted
50 g (2 oz) caster sugar
175 g (6 oz) shortcake biscuits,
crushed
For the filling
227 g (8 oz) carton curd cheese
3 eggs, separated
4 tbls golden syrup, warmed
25 g (1 oz) plain flour, sifted
6 tbls double or whipping cream
50 g (2 oz) caster sugar
75 g (3 oz) blanched almonds,
chopped
For the topping
142 ml (5 fl oz) carton soured cream
25 g (1 oz) flaked almonds, toasted

Heat the oven to 160°C, 325°F, Gas Mark 3. Grease a loose-bottomed or spring-form 18-20 cm (7-8 inch) tin.

Mix the melted margarine with the sugar and biscuit crumbs. Spoon into the greased tin and press evenly over base. Chill while making filling.

Beat the cheese in a bowl until softened. Beat in the egg yolks, syrup, flour and cream. Whisk the egg whites until stiff, then whisk in the sugar. Fold into the cheese mixture, with the chopped almonds. Turn into the tin and smooth the surface.

Place the cheesecake on a baking sheet and bake in the oven for 1½-1¾ hours or until set. Cool for 1 hour.

Run a round-bladed knife around the sides of the cheesecake, then transfer to a plate and spread the soured cream over the top. Chill for 2-3 hours then decorate with almonds.

Variation: For Almond liqueur cheesecake, stir 1-2 tsp Amaretto into the soured cream topping before spreading it over the cheesecake. Decorate with halved glacé cherries and toasted flaked almonds.

● Duchess cheesecake; Apricot cheesecake

Spiced pear cheesecake

SERVES 8

For the base
75g (3oz) margarine or butter, melted
50g (2oz) caster sugar
pinch of ground mixed spice
175g (6oz) digestive biscuits, crushed
For the filling
227g (8oz) carton curd cheese
3 eggs, separated
½ tsp ground mixed spice
100g (4oz) caster sugar
grated rind of ½ lemon
1 tbls lemon juice
2 pears, peeled, cored, finely chopped
40g (1½oz) plain flour, sifted
75g (3oz) Cheddar cheese, grated
6 tbls soured cream
To decorate
4 canned pear halves, drained
angelica, chopped
142 ml (5 fl oz) carton double cream,
    whipped

Heat the oven to 160°C, 325°F, Gas Mark 3. Grease a loose-bottomed or spring-form 18-20 cm (7-8 inch) cake tin.

Mix the melted margarine with the sugar, spice and biscuit crumbs. Spoon into tin and press evenly over base. Chill while making filling.

Beat the cheese in a bowl. Beat in egg yolks, spice, 50g (2oz) sugar, lemon rind and juice, chopped pears, flour, grated cheese and soured cream.

Whisk the egg whites until stiff, then whisk in remaining sugar. Fold lightly, but thoroughly, into cheese mixture. Turn into the prepared tin and smooth the surface.

Place the cheesecake on a baking sheet and bake in the oven for 1½-1¾ hours, or until the filling is set. Leave the cheesecake to cool for 1 hour.

Run a round-bladed knife around the sides of the cheesecake, then transfer to a plate and decorate with pear halves, angelica, and piped cream. Chill for 2-3 hours before serving.

Deluxe ginger cheesecake

SERVES 8

For the base
75g (3oz) margarine or butter, melted
50g (2oz) caster sugar
175g (6oz) gingernuts, crushed
For the filling
300g (10oz) curd cheese
3 eggs, separated
3 tbls black treacle, warmed
50g (2oz) soft light brown sugar
grated rind of ½ lemon
1 tbls lemon juice
25g (1oz) plain flour, sifted
2 tsp ground ginger
6 tbls soured cream
50g (2oz) caster sugar
75g (3oz) crystallized ginger,
    chopped
To decorate
142 ml (5 fl oz) carton double or
    whipping cream, lightly whipped
4 pieces stem ginger, chopped

Heat the oven to 160°C, 325°F, Gas Mark 3. Grease a loose-bottomed or spring-form 18-20 cm (7-8 inch) cake tin.

Mix the melted margarine with the sugar and biscuit crumbs. Spoon into tin and press evenly over base. Chill.

Beat the cheese in a bowl until softened. Beat in the egg yolks, treacle, brown sugar, lemon rind and juice, flour, ginger and soured cream.

Whisk the egg whites until stiff, then whisk in the caster sugar. Using a large metal spoon, fold lightly, but thoroughly, into the cheese mixture, together with the chopped crystallized ginger. Turn into prepared tin and smooth the surface.

Place the cheesecake on a baking sheet and bake in the oven for 1½-1¾ hours, or until set. Cool for 1 hour.

Run a round-bladed knife around the sides of the cheesecake, then transfer to a plate. Pipe cream over top and decorate with stem ginger. Chill for 2-3 hours before serving.

• Spiced pear cheesecake; Deluxe ginger cheesecake

Tutti frutti cheesecake

SERVES 8

For the base
75 g (3 oz) margarine or butter, melted
175 g (6 oz) digestive biscuits, crushed
For the filling
500 g (1 1/4 lb) curd cheese
75 g (3 oz) caster sugar
4 eggs, beaten
grated rind of 2 lemons
50 g (2 oz) sultanas
25 g (1 oz) glacé cherries, chopped
25 g (1 oz) glacé pineapple, chopped
50 g (2 oz) cut mixed peel
1 tbls cornflour
2 tbls lemon juice
For the topping
142 ml (5 fl oz) carton soured cream
2 tsp caster sugar
1/2 tsp vanilla essence
shredded lemon zest, to decorate

Heat the oven to 180°C, 350°F, Gas Mark 4. Grease a 23 cm (9 inch) loose-bottomed or spring-form cake tin. Mix the melted margarine with the biscuit crumbs. Spoon into the greased tin and press evenly over the base. Chill in the refrigerator while making the tutti frutti filling.

Beat the cheese and sugar together in a bowl. Gradually beat in the eggs, then stir in the lemon rind, fruit and peel. Blend the cornflour with the lemon juice to make a smooth paste and stir into the cheese mixture.

Turn the mixture into the prepared tin and smooth the surface. Place the cheesecake on a baking sheet and bake in the oven for 20 minutes, or until the filling is just set.

To make the topping, blend the soured cream with the sugar and vanilla essence.

Remove the cheesecake from the oven and spread the soured cream mixture over the surface of the cake. Return to the oven for a further 5 minutes.

Leave the cheesecake for 3-4 hours, until cold, then chill in the refrigerator overnight. Run a round-bladed knife around the sides of the cheesecake, then remove from the tin.

Transfer the cheesecake to a serving plate and decorate with lemon zest.

Variation: For Fruit 'n' nut cheesecake, replace the glacé pineapple with coarsely chopped walnuts. Decorate with halved glacé cherries and 'diamonds' of angelica.

● Tutti frutti cheesecake

Cheesecake pudding

SERVES 6

227 g (8 oz) carton cottage cheese,
   sieved
175 g (6 oz) caster sugar
2 eggs, separated
grated rind of 1 lemon
100 g (4 oz) plain flour
1 tsp baking powder
75 g (3 oz) seedless raisins
50 g (2 oz) blanched almonds,
   chopped
icing sugar, for dusting (optional)

● Cheesecake pudding

Heat the oven to 180°C, 350°F, Gas
Mark 4. Grease a 20 cm (8 inch) pie dish
or ovenproof serving dish.
   Put the cheese in a mixing bowl. Add
the caster sugar, egg yolks and lemon
rind. Sift in the flour with the baking
powder and beat well until the mixture
is thoroughly blended.
   Whisk the egg whites until stiff.
Using a large metal spoon, fold lightly,
but thoroughly, into the cheese mixture. Fold in the raisins and almonds.
Turn the mixture into the greased pie
dish and smooth the surface with a
palette knife.

Bake in the oven for about 45 minutes, or until a fine skewer inserted into
the centre of the cheesecake pudding
comes out clean.
   Leave to cool for 3-4 hours, or until
cold, then sift icing sugar over the top, if
using. Serve straight from the dish.

Serving ideas: This dessert is even
more delicious accompanied by a bowl
of sugared strawberries or raspberries,
a cold fruit compôte, or fruit sauce.
Variation: For Rum and raisin cheesecake pudding, add 1 tbls dark rum with
the egg yolks, sugar and lemon rind.

Cherry cheesecake

SERVES 8

For the base
100 g (4 oz) plain flour
25 g (1 oz) icing sugar
75 g (3 oz) margarine or butter,
    softened
1 egg yolk
For the filling
227 g (8 oz) carton curd cheese
3 eggs, separated
½ tsp ground cinnamon
100 g (4 oz) caster sugar
25 g (1 oz) plain flour, sifted
142 ml (5 fl oz) carton double cream
425 g (15 oz) can stoned red cherries,
    drained
For the topping
397 g (14 oz) can cherry pie filling
142 ml (5 fl oz) whipping cream,
    whipped

Heat the oven to 160°C, 325°F, Gas
Mark 3. Grease a loose-bottomed or
spring-form 18-20 cm (7-8 inch) tin.

Sift the flour and icing sugar into a
mixing bowl. Add the margarine and
egg yolk and work to a soft dough.

Shape the dough into a ball, then
press evenly over the base of the greased
tin. Chill while making the filling.

Beat the cheese in a bowl until softened. Beat in the egg yolks, cinnamon,
50 g (2 oz) of the sugar, the flour and
cream. Whisk the egg whites until stiff,
then whisk in the remaining sugar.
Fold lightly, but thoroughly, into the
cheese mixture.

Scatter the cherries over the pastry
base. Spoon the cheese mixture on top
and smooth the surface.

Bake in the oven for 1½-1¾ hours, or
until the filling is set. Leave the cheesecake to cool for 1 hour.

Run a round-bladed knife around
the sides of the cheesecake, then transfer to a plate and top with pie filling and
piped cream. Chill for 2-3 hours in the
refrigerator before serving.

Redcurrant cheese tartlets

SERVES 6

For the base
225 g (8 oz) plain flour
pinch of salt
50 g (2 oz) margarine or butter, diced
50 g (2 oz) lard, diced
8 tsp cold water
For the filling
175 g (6 oz) full fat soft cheese
100 g (4 oz) caster sugar
2 eggs, separated
6 tbls redcurrant jelly
2 tbls double or whipping cream
fresh redcurrants, to decorate

Sift the flour with the salt into a mixing
bowl. Add the margarine and lard and
rub in with the fingertips until the mixture resembles fine breadcrumbs.
Sprinkle over the water and mix it in
with a round-bladed knife. Draw the
mixture together to make a firm dough,
adding a little more water if too dry.

Turn the dough on to a lightly floured
surface and knead lightly for 1 minute
until smooth. Wrap in foil or cling film
and chill for 20-30 minutes.

Heat the oven to 190°C, 375°F, Gas
Mark 5. Roll out the dough on a lightly
floured surface and use to line 6 indi-
vidual large tartlet tins. Prick each base
with a fork. Chill while making filling.

Beat the cheese in a bowl. Beat in half
the caster sugar, the egg yolks, 2 tbls
redcurrant jelly and the cream.

Whisk the egg whites until stiff, then
whisk in the remaining caster sugar.
Fold into the cheese mixture and divide
among the pastry cases.

Bake in the oven for 25-30 minutes
or until the filling is set. Cool for 3-4
hours.

Melt the remaining redcurrant jelly
in a small saucepan over low heat.
Spoon jelly over each tartlet. Leave until
set. Decorate with redcurrants.

● Cherry cheesecake; Redcurrant cheese tartlets

Luxury chocolate cheesecake

SERVES 6-8

For the base
65 g (2½ oz) plain flour
pinch of salt
25 g (1 oz) walnuts, finely ground
25 g (1 oz) caster sugar
25 g (1 oz) unsalted butter, diced
1-2 tsp cold water
For the filling
75 g (3 oz) plain dessert chocolate
450 g (1 lb) full fat soft cheese
150 g (5 oz) caster sugar
2 tbls plain flour, sifted
3 eggs, separated
*284 ml (10 fl oz) carton whipping
   cream*
chocolate scrolls, to decorate

Sift the flour with the salt into a mixing bowl. Stir in the ground walnuts and sugar. Add the butter and rub it in with the fingertips until the mixture resembles coarse breadcrumbs.

Sprinkle over the water and draw the mixture together to make a firm dough.

Turn the dough on to a lightly floured surface and knead lightly for 1 minute, until smooth. Shape into a ball, wrap in foil and chill for 20 minutes.

Heat the oven to 200°C, 400°F, Gas Mark 6. Grease the base of a 20 cm (8 inch) loose-bottomed cake tin. Place the dough on the tin base and roll it out to cover. Trim the edges and prick the dough all over with a fork. Bake in the oven for 15 minutes, or until golden. Leave on a wire rack until cold.

Grease the side of the tin and attach to the base. Reduce the oven heat to 160°C, 325°F, Gas Mark 3.

To make the filling, break the chocolate into pieces and place in a heatproof bowl set over a saucepan of hot water. Heat gently, stirring occasionally, until melted. Remove from the heat.

Beat the cheese in a bowl. Beat in the sugar, flour, egg yolks, chocolate and 75 ml (3 fl oz) of the cream.

Whisk the egg whites until stiff. Using a large metal spoon, fold one-third of the egg whites into the cheese mixture, then fold in the remainder. Turn into prepared tin on a baking sheet.

Bake in the oven for 1 hour, or until the filling is set. Leave the cheesecake for 3-4 hours, then chill overnight.

Run a round-bladed knife around the sides of the cheesecake, then remove from the tin. Transfer the cheesecake to a serving plate. Whip the remaining cream and swirl over the top of the cheesecake. Decorate with chocolate scrolls.

● Bottom left: Luxury chocolate cheesecake; Top: Yuletide cheesecake

Yuletide cheesecake

SERVES 8-10

For the base
50g (2oz) margarine or butter, melted
50g (2oz) caster sugar
175g (6oz) ratafias, crushed
1 tbls dark rum
For the filling
350g (12oz) full fat soft cheese
3 eggs, separated
good pinch of ground mixed spice
a few drops of rum essence
100g (4oz) caster sugar
25g (1oz) plain flour, sifted
1 tbls ground almonds
142 ml (5 fl oz) carton double or
   whipping cream
50g (2oz) cut mixed peel
50g (2oz) glacé cherries, chopped
25g (1oz) sultanas
25g (1oz) nuts, chopped
grated rind of 1 orange
For the icing and decoration
225g (8oz) icing sugar
1 egg white, lightly whisked
holly sprig decoration

Heat the oven to 160°C, 325°F, Gas
Mark 3. Grease a loose-bottomed or
spring-form 18-20 cm (7-8 inch) cake
tin.

Mix the melted margarine with the
sugar, ratafia crumbs and rum. Spoon
into the greased tin and press evenly
over the base. Chill in the refrigerator
while making the filling.

Beat the cheese in a bowl until softened. Beat in the egg yolks, spice, rum
essence, half the sugar, the flour,
ground almonds and cream.

Whisk the egg whites until stiff, then
whisk in the remaining sugar. Using a
large metal spoon, fold lightly, but thoroughly, into the cheese mixture,
together with the peel, fruit, nuts and
orange rind. Turn the mixture into the
prepared tin and smooth the surface.

Place the cheesecake on a baking
sheet and bake in the oven for 1½-1¾
hours or until the filling is set. Leave the
cheesecake to cool for 1 hour.

Run a round-bladed knife around
the sides of the cheesecake, then remove from the tin. Transfer the cheesecake to a wire rack.

To make the icing, sift the icing
sugar into a mixing bowl, then beat in
the egg white. Spread the icing over the
top and sides of the cheesecake, peak-
ing it decoratively. Leave until the icing
is just beginning to set, then add the
holly sprig decoration. Leave for a
further 2-3 hours, or until completely
set, before serving.

Serving ideas: This cheesecake is an
attractive alternative to traditional
Christmas cake.

Rich lemon cheesecake

SERVES 6

For the base
50 g (2 oz) margarine or butter, melted
25 g (1 oz) soft dark brown sugar
100 g (4 oz) chocolate digestive
*   biscuits, crushed*
For the filling
15 g (½ oz) sachet powdered gelatine
2 tbls water
350 g (12 oz) full fat soft cheese
75 g (3 oz) caster sugar
grated rind of 1 lemon
4 tbls lemon juice
142 ml (5 fl oz) carton double cream
crystallized lemon slices, to decorate

Grease an 18 cm (7 inch) flan ring on a baking sheet. Mix the melted margarine with the sugar and biscuit crumbs. Spoon into the greased flan tin and press evenly over the base and sides. Chill while making the filling.

Sprinkle the gelatine over the water in a small heatproof bowl and leave for 2-3 minutes until spongy. Stand the bowl in a pan of hot water and stir until the gelatine has dissolved. Set aside to cool slightly.

Place the cheese, sugar, lemon rind and juice in a mixing bowl and beat until smooth, then beat in the liquid gelatine.

Whip the cream until it forms soft peaks, then fold into the cheese mixture. Turn into the prepared flan ring and smooth the surface. Chill in the refrigerator for 3-4 hours, or until set.

Remove the cheesecake from the ring and transfer to a serving plate. Decorate with lemon slices. Serve the cheesecake chilled.

Raspberry princess cheesecake

SERVES 8

For the base
100 g (4 oz) margarine or butter,
*   melted*
225 g (8 oz) digestive biscuits, crushed
For the filling
15 g (½ oz) sachet powdered gelatine
3 tbls water
450 g (1 lb) full fat soft cheese
50 g (2 oz) caster sugar
2 egg yolks
225 g (8 oz) raspberries
142 ml (5 fl oz) carton double or
*   whipping cream*

Lightly grease a loose-bottomed or spring-form 20cm (8 inch) cake tin.

Mix the melted margarine with the biscuit crumbs. Spoon into the greased tin and press evenly over the base. Chill while making the filling.

Sprinkle the gelatine over the water in a small heatproof bowl and leave for 2-3 minutes until spongy. Stand the bowl in a pan of hot water and stir until dissolved. Set aside to cool slightly.

Place the cheese, caster sugar and the egg yolks in a mixing bowl with 175 g (6 oz) of the raspberries and beat well until thoroughly blended. Stir in the liquid gelatine. Whip the cream until it forms soft peaks, then fold into the mixture.

Turn the mixture into the prepared tin and chill for 3-4 hours, or until set.

Run a round-bladed knife around the sides of the cheesecake, then remove from tin. Transfer to a plate. Decorate with remaining raspberries.

● Rich lemon cheesecake; Raspberry princess cheesecake

Carnival cheesecake

SERVES 10-12

For the base
*100 g (4 oz) margarine or butter,
    melted*
100 g (4 oz) caster sugar
225 g (8 oz) coconut cookies, crushed
For the filling
*3 × 15 g (½ oz) sachets powdered
    gelatine*
*200 ml (7 fl oz) unsweetened
    pineapple juice*
450 g (1 lb) full fat soft cheese
300 g (11 oz) caster sugar
4 eggs, separated
*284 ml (10 fl oz) carton double
    cream*
*425 g (15 oz) can mango pieces,
    drained and chopped, syrup
    reserved*
100 g (4 oz) walnuts, chopped
To decorate
*450 ml (¾ pint) double cream,
    whipped*
4 kiwi fruit, thinly sliced
walnut halves

Lightly grease a loose-bottomed or spring-form 25-30 cm (10-12 inch) cake tin.

Mix the melted margarine with the sugar and coconut cookie crumbs. Spoon into the greased tin and press evenly over the base. Chill in the refrigerator while making the filling.

Sprinkle the gelatine over the pineapple juice in a small heatproof bowl and leave for 2-3 minutes until spongy. Stand the bowl in a pan of hot water and stir until the gelatine has dissolved. Remove from the heat and set the liquid gelatine aside to cool slightly while making the filling.

Beat the cheese in a bowl until softened. Beat in 100 g (4 oz) of the sugar, the egg yolks and cream. Stir in the liquid gelatine. Set the mixture aside until it is on the point of setting. Whisk the egg whites until stiff, then whisk in 100 g (4 oz) of the remaining sugar. Using a large metal spoon, fold lightly, but thoroughly, into the cheese mixture

together with the chopped mango and walnuts. Turn the mixture into the prepared tin and gently tip and tilt it to level the surface. Chill in the refrigerator for 3-4 hours, or until set.

Meanwhile, put the reserved mango syrup and the remaining sugar into a small saucepan and stir over low heat until the sugar has dissolved. Bring to the boil and boil for 1 minute, then remove from the heat and leave to cool.

Run a round-bladed knife around the sides of the cheesecake, then remove from the tin. Transfer the cheesecake to a serving plate.

Thinly spread some of the whipped cream around the sides of the cheesecake. Spread or pipe the remaining cream round the edge and decorate with kiwi slices and walnuts. Brush the fruit and nuts with the cooled mango syrup.

Fresh lime cheesecake

SERVES 8

For the base
50 g (2 oz) margarine or butter, melted
50 g (2 oz) caster sugar
100 g (4 oz) wafer biscuits, crushed
For the filling
juice of 2 limes
3 tbls water
15 g (½ oz) sachet powdered gelatine
225 g (8 oz) full fat soft cheese
2 eggs, separated
100 g (4 oz) caster sugar
grated rind of 6 limes
*142 ml (5 fl oz) carton double or
    whipping cream*
To decorate
*142 ml (5 fl oz) carton double or
    whipping cream*
lime slices, halved

Lightly grease a loose-bottomed or spring-form 18-20 cm (7-8 inch) cake tin.

Mix the melted margarine with the sugar and biscuit crumbs. Spoon into the greased tin and press evenly over the base. Chill in the refrigerator while making the filling.

Pour the lime juice into a small heat-proof bowl. Add the water, then sprinkle over the gelatine and leave for 2-3 minutes until spongy. Stand the bowl in a pan of hot water and stir until the gelatine has dissolved. Set aside to cool slightly.

Beat the cheese in a bowl until softened. Beat in the egg yolks, half the sugar, the lime rind and the cream. Stir in the liquid gelatine. Leave the mixture until it is on the point of setting.

Whisk the egg whites until stiff, then whisk in the remaining sugar. Using a large metal spoon, fold lightly, but thoroughly, into the cheese mixture.

Turn the mixture into the prepared tin and gently tilt and tip it to level the surface. Chill in the refrigerator for 3-4 hours, or until set.

Run 'a round-bladed knife around the sides of the cheesecake, then remove from the tin. Transfer the cheesecake to a serving plate. Whip the remaining cream until it forms soft peaks, then pipe or spread round the edge of the cheesecake. Decorate with lime slices.

Variations: Omit the decoration. Place 4 tbls lime marmalade in a saucepan with 1 tbls lime juice and warm gently until the marmalade has melted. Cool slightly, then spread over the top of the cheesecake.

For Lemon 'n' lime cheesecake, use the juice of 1 lime and ½ lemon and grated rind of 4 limes and 1 lemon. Decorate with lemon and lime twists.

• Carnival cheesecake; Fresh lime cheesecake

Upside-down pineapple cheesecake

SERVES 8

For the base
50 g (2 oz) margarine or butter, melted
50 g (2 oz) soft light brown sugar
100 g (4 oz) gingernut biscuits,
  crushed
For the filling
15 g (½ oz) sachet powdered gelatine
5 tbls unsweetened pineapple juice
225 g (8 oz) full fat soft cheese
2 eggs, separated
100 g (4 oz) caster sugar
grated rind of ½ lemon
142 ml (5 fl oz) carton soured cream
For the topping
4 small canned pineapple rings
5 maraschino or glacé cherries
142 ml (5 fl oz) double or whipping
  cream, whipped
angelica 'diamonds', to decorate

Lightly grease a loose-bottomed or spring-form 18-20 cm (7-8 inch) cake tin.

Mix the melted margarine with the sugar and biscuit crumbs. Spoon into a bowl and chill in the refrigerator while making the filling.

Sprinkle the gelatine over the pineapple juice in a small heatproof bowl and leave until spongy. Stand the bowl in a pan of hot water and stir until the gelatine has dissolved. Set aside to cool slightly.

Beat the cheese in a bowl until softened. Beat in the egg yolks, half the sugar, the lemon rind and soured cream. Stir in the liquid gelatine. Leave the mixture until it is just on the point of setting.

Whisk the egg whites until stiff, then whisk in the remaining sugar. Using a large metal spoon, fold lightly, but thoroughly, into the cheese and gelatine mixture.

To make the topping, arrange the pineapple rings in the base of the greased tin. Put a cherry in the centre of each ring.

Turn the cheese mixture into the prepared tin and smooth the surface. Sprinkle the biscuit-crumb mixture evenly over the top and press down lightly with the back of a metal spoon. Chill in the refrigerator for 3-4 hours.

Run a round-bladed knife around the sides of the cheesecake, then remove from the tin. Transfer the cheesecake to a serving plate. Slide a round-bladed knife between the base of the tin and the topping, then lift off the tin base. Pipe two rings of whipped cream round the cheesecake, place a cherry in the centre, and decorate with angelica 'diamonds'.

Variations: For Upside-down peach or pear cheesecake, used drained canned peach or pear halves instead of pineapple rings. Place a maraschino cherry in the cavity of each fruit, then arrange the fruit cut side down on the base of the tin. Omit the angelica and sprinkle chopped walnuts in between the fruit. Spread the sides of the cheesecake with cream and coat with 100 g (4 oz) chopped walnuts or toasted almonds.

Mellow-mallow cheesecake

SERVES 8

For the base
18-20 cm (7-8 inch) sponge cake layer,
  1 cm (½ inch) thick
For the filling
175 g (6 oz) marshmallows
3 tbls milk
15 g (½ oz) sachet powdered gelatine
3 tbls water
225 g (8 oz) full fat soft cheese
2 eggs, separated
100 g (4 oz) caster sugar
6 tbls soured cream
To decorate
75 g (3 oz) marshmallows, halved

Lightly grease a loose-bottomed or spring-form 18-20 cm (7-8 inch) cake tin. Place the sponge cake in the greased tin, trimming it round the edge

● Upside-down pineapple cheesecake; Mellow-mallow cheesecake

if necessary to fit exactly.

To make the filling, snip the marshmallows into pieces with lightly oiled kitchen scissors and place in a saucepan with the milk. Stir over low heat until the marshmallows have melted. Remove from the heat and reserve.

Sprinkle the gelatine over the water in a small heatproof bowl and leave for 2-3 minutes until spongy. Stand the bowl in a pan of hot water and stir until the gelatine has dissolved. Set aside to cool slightly.

Beat the cheese in a bowl until softened. Beat in the egg yolks, half the caster sugar, the melted marshmallows and the soured cream. Stir in the liquid gelatine. Leave the mixture until it is on the point of setting.

Whisk the egg whites until stiff, then whisk in the remaining sugar. Using a large metal spoon, fold lightly, but

thoroughly, into the cheese mixture.

Turn the mixture into the prepared tin and gently tilt and tip it to level the surface. Chill for 3-4 hours.

Run a round-bladed knife around the sides of the cheesecake, then remove from the tin. Transfer the cheesecake to a serving plate.

To decorate press the halved marshmallows, cut side down, around the edge of the cheesecake.

Variations: The marshmallow topping may be drizzled with melted chocolate.

For a Chocolate mallow cheesecake, mix 100 g (4 oz) crushed bourbon biscuits with 50 g (2 oz) melted margarine or butter and use for the base instead of the sponge cake.

For a Ginger mallow cheesecake, use 100 g (4 oz) crushed gingernut biscuits in the same way.

Banana cheesecake

SERVES 8

For the base
50 g (2 oz) margarine or butter, melted
50 g (2 oz) caster sugar
100 g (4 oz) chocolate digestive
biscuits, crushed
For the filling
15 g (½ oz) sachet powdered gelatine
3 tbls water
2 ripe bananas
grated rind of ½ lemon
2 tbls lemon juice
100 g (4 oz) caster sugar
225 g (8 oz) full fat soft cheese
2 eggs, separated
142 ml (5 fl oz) carton soured cream
To decorate
2 small bananas
2 tbls lemon juice
50 g (2 oz) plain chocolate, melted

Grease a loose-bottomed or spring-form 18-20 cm (7-8 inch) cake tin.

Mix the melted margarine with the sugar and biscuit crumbs. Spoon into the greased tin and press evenly over the base. Chill in the refrigerator while making the filling.

Sprinkle the gelatine over the water in a small heatproof bowl and leave for 2-3 minutes until spongy. Stand the bowl in a pan of hot water and stir until the gelatine has dissolved. Set aside to cool slightly.

Peel and mash the bananas with the lemon rind and juice and half the sugar until smooth. Beat in the cheese, egg yolks and soured cream. Stir in the liquid gelatine. Leave the mixture until it is on the point of setting.

Whisk the egg whites until stiff, then whisk in the remaining caster sugar. Fold lightly, but thoroughly, into the cheese mixture.

Turn the mixture into the prepared tin and gently tilt and tip it to level the surface. Chill in the refrigerator for 3-4 hours, or until set.

Run a round-bladed knife around the sides of the cheesecake, then remove from the tin. Transfer the cheese-cake to a serving plate. Thinly slice the bananas and dip them immediately in lemon juice to prevent them from dis-colouring. Pat dry with absorbent paper and dip half each banana slice in the melted chocolate. Leave until the chocolate is set, then arrange round the edge of the cheesecake.

Variation: For Crunchy banana cheesecake, make the base with muesli instead of chocolate digestive biscuits. Include coarsely crushed sesame snaps or toasted flaked almonds in the decoration.

Marmalade cheesecake

SERVES 8

For the base
25 g (1 oz) margarine or butter
50 g (2 oz) caster sugar
3 tbls jelly marmalade
100 g (4 oz) digestive biscuits,
crushed
For the filling and decoration
15 g (½ oz) sachet powdered
gelatine
3 tbls water
225 g (8 oz) full fat soft cheese
grated rind of 2 oranges
2 eggs, separated
100 g (4 oz) caster sugar
3 tbls coarse-cut marmalade
142 ml (5 fl oz) carton soured cream
fresh orange segments, peeled, to
decorate
3 tbls jelly marmalade, to glaze

Grease a loose-bottomed or spring-form 18-20 cm (7-8 inch) cake tin.

Melt the margarine with the sugar and marmalade in a saucepan over low heat. Remove from the heat and stir in the biscuit crumbs. Spoon into the greased tin and press evenly over the base. Chill in the refrigerator while making the filling.

Sprinkle the gelatine over the water in a small heatproof bowl and leave for 2-3 minutes until spongy. Stand the bowl in a pan of hot water and stir until the gelatine has dissolved. Set aside to cool slightly.

Place the cheese in a mixing bowl with the orange rind and beat until softened. Beat in the egg yolks, half the sugar, the coarse-cut marmalade and soured cream. Stir in the liquid gelatine. Set the mixture aside until it is on the point of setting.

Whisk the egg whites until stiff, then whisk in the remaining sugar. Using a large metal spoon, fold lightly, but thoroughly, into the cheese mixture.

Turn the mixture into the prepared tin and gently tip and tilt it to level the surface. Chill in the refrigerator for 3-4 hours, or until set.

Run a round-bladed knife around the sides of the cheesecake, then remove from the tin. Arrange the orange segments on top of the cheesecake. Warm the jelly marmalade in a small saucepan until melted and smooth; cool slightly, then spoon over the orange segments.

Transfer the cheesecake to a serving plate. Chill in the refrigerator for 15-20 minutes to set the marmalade glaze before serving.

Variation

For Paddington's cheesecake, to serve for a children's afternoon tea, use sieved cottage cheese instead of full fat cheese and orange yoghurt in place of soured cream.

For a Lime marmalade cheesecake, use lime rind and juice instead of orange, lime marmalade instead of orange, and lime twists to decorate.

● Top: Marmalade cheesecake; Bottom: Banana cheesecake

Dreamy midsummer's cheesecake

SERVES 8

For the base
50g (2oz) margarine or butter, melted
50g (2oz) caster sugar
100g (4oz) ratafias or macaroons,
   crushed
For the filling
15g (½oz) sachet powdered gelatine
3 tbls water
225g (8oz) full fat soft cheese
2 eggs, separated
100g (4oz) caster sugar
grated rind of 1 orange
a few drops of almond essence
142 ml (5 fl oz) carton double or
   whipping cream
To decorate
225-350g (8-12oz) mixed
   strawberries, cherries or raspberries
   and redcurrants
3 tbls redcurrant jelly
1 tbls strained orange juice

Grease a loose-bottomed or spring-form 18-20 cm (7-8 inch) cake tin.

Mix the melted margarine with the sugar and ratafia crumbs. Spoon into the greased tin and press evenly over the base. Chill the biscuit base in the refrigerator while making the almond-flavoured filling.

Sprinkle the gelatine over the water in a heatproof bowl and leave for 2-3 minutes until spongy. Stand the bowl in a pan of hot water and stir until the gelatine has dissolved. Set the liquid gelatine aside to cool slightly.

Beat the cheese in a bowl until softened. Beat in the egg yolks, half the sugar, the orange rind, almond essence and cream. Stir in the liquid gelatine. Leave the mixture until it is on the point of setting.

Whisk the egg whites until stiff, then whisk in the remaining caster sugar. Using a large metal spoon, fold lightly, but thoroughly, into the cheese mixture.

Turn the mixture into the prepared tin and gently tilt and tip it to level the surface. Chill in the refrigerator for 3-4 hours, or until set.

Run a round-bladed knife around the sides of the cheesecake, then remove from the tin. Arrange the fruit over the top of the cheesecake. Melt the jelly with the orange juice in a small saucepan over low heat; cool slightly, then brush or spoon over the fruit. Transfer the cheesecake to a serving plate. Allow the glaze to set before serving the cheesecake well chilled.

Exotic cheesecake gâteau

SERVES 4-6

For the sponge base
50 g (2 oz) self-raising flour
½ tsp baking powder
50 g (2 oz) caster sugar
50 g (2 oz) butter, softened
1 egg, lightly beaten
For the filling and decoration
15 g (½ oz) sachet powdered gelatine
3 tbls water
350 g (12 oz) curd cheese
75 g (3 oz) caster sugar
1 tsp vanilla essence
3 egg whites
284 ml (10 fl oz) carton double cream
3 kiwi fruit, sliced
1 tbls icing sugar

Heat oven to 180°C, 350°F, Gas Mark 4. Grease an 18 cm (7 inch) sandwich tin. Line base with greased greaseproof.

To make the sponge base, sift the flour with the baking powder into a mixing bowl. Add the sugar, butter and egg and beat together with a wooden spoon for 1-2 minutes, or with a hand-held electric whisk for 1 minute, until thoroughly blended.

Turn into the tin and smooth the surface. Bake in the oven for about 20 minutes, until firm to the touch. Cool the sponge for 1 minute, then turn on to a wire rack and carefully peel off the

● Bottom: Dreamy midsummer's cheesecake; Top: Exotic cheesecake gâteau

lining paper. Leave to cool completely.

Sprinkle the gelatine over the water in a small heatproof bowl and leave for 2-3 minutes until spongy. Stand the bowl in a pan of hot water and stir until dissolved. Set aside to cool slightly.

Beat the cheese in a bowl. Stir in the sugar, vanilla and liquid gelatine.

Whisk the egg whites until stiff. In a separate bowl, whip the cream until it forms soft peaks. Reserve one-third of the cream for decoration. Fold the remaining cream into the cheese mixture, then fold in the egg whites.

Lightly oil the sides of a loose-bottomed or spring-form 18 cm (7 inch) cake tin. Split the sponge base in half horizontally and place the bottom layer in the tin base. Top with half the kiwi fruit. Pour in the cheese mixture, then place the remaining sponge layer on top. Chill for 3-4 hours, or until set.

Run a round-bladed knife around the sides of the cheesecake, then remove from the tin. Sift the icing sugar over the top. Transfer to a plate. Pipe cream on top and decorate.

Topsy turvy cheesecake

SERVES 6-8

For the filling
227 g (8 oz) carton cottage cheese
4 tsp fresh orange juice
2 eggs, separated
100 g (4 oz) caster sugar
grated rind of 1 orange
15 g (½ oz) sachet powdered gelatine
3 tbls water
100 ml (3½ fl oz) double cream,
  whipped
For the base
40 g (1½ oz) margarine or butter,
  melted
1 tbls demerara sugar
75 g (3 oz) digestive biscuits, crushed
To decorate
225 g (8 oz) strawberries, hulled
orange twists

Grease a 20 cm (8 inch) sandwich tin.

To make the filling, process the cheese and orange juice smoothly in a blender.

Place the egg yolks, sugar and orange rind in a mixing bowl and whisk until light and creamy. Whisk in the cheese and orange mixture.

Sprinkle the gelatine over the water in a small heatproof bowl and leave for 2-3 minutes until spongy. Stand the bowl in a pan of hot water and stir until the gelatine has dissolved. Set aside to cool slightly, then whisk the liquid gelatine into the cheese mixture.

Whisk the egg whites until just stiff.

Fold the cream into the cheese mixture, then fold in the whisked egg whites. Turn the mixture into the greased tin and smooth the surface. Chill for 3-4 hours, until set.

To make the base, mix the melted margarine with the sugar and biscuit crumbs. Spread evenly over the surface of the cheese mixture, pressing down

• Liqueur cheesepots; Dark chocolate cheesecake; Topsy turvy cheesecake

gently with the back of a large metal spoon. Chill in the refrigerator for 20-30 minutes or until firm.

To turn out the cheesecake, run a round-bladed knife around the sides. Dip the base of the tin in warm water for 1-2 seconds, then invert a serving plate on top of the tin. Hold the plate and tin firmly together and invert, then lift away the tin.

Decorate the cheesecake with the strawberries and orange twists.

Dark chocolate cheesecake

SERVES 10-12

For the base
100g (4oz) margarine, melted
100g (4oz) soft dark brown sugar
225g (8oz) chocolate digestive
  biscuits, crushed
For the filling
100g (4oz) ratafias
6 tbls dark rum
2 × 15g (½oz) sachets powdered
  gelatine
6 tbls water
450g (1 lb) full fat soft cheese
4 eggs, separated
225g (8oz) soft dark brown sugar
2 tbls drinking chocolate powder
3 tbls hot water
284 ml (10 fl oz) carton double cream
To decorate
75g (3oz) plain dessert chocolate
285 ml (10 fl oz) carton double cream
1 tbls dark rum

Lightly grease a loose-bottomed or spring-form 25-30 cm (10-12 inch) tin.

Mix the melted margarine with the sugar and biscuit crumbs. Spoon into the greased tin and press evenly over the base. Chill while making the filling.

Reserve a few ratafias for decoration. Put the remaining ratafias into a bowl and sprinkle with the rum. Cover and leave to one side.

Sprinkle the gelatine over the water in a small heatproof bowl and leave for 2-3 minutes until spongy. Stand the bowl in a pan of hot water and stir until dissolved. Leave to cool slightly.

Beat the cheese in a bowl until softened. Beat in the egg yolks and half the sugar. Dissolve the drinking chocolate in the hot water, allow to cool slightly then beat into the cheese mixture together with the cream. Stir in the liquid gelatine. Leave the mixture until it is on the point of setting.

Whisk the egg whites until stiff, then whisk in the remaining sugar. Using a large metal spoon, fold lightly, but thoroughly, into the cheese mixture.

Spoon half the mixture into the prepared tin and smooth the surface. Spoon the rum-soaked ratafias over the top. Cover with the remaining cheese mixture. Gently tilt and tip tin to level surface. Chill for 3-4 hours.

Meanwhile, prepare the decoration. Using a potato peeler, shave the chocolate into curls or flakes. Whip the cream with the rum until it forms soft peaks.

Run a round-bladed knife around the sides of the cheesecake, then remove from the tin. Transfer the cheesecake to a serving plate. Pipe or swirl the cream over the top. Decorate with the reserved ratafias and chocolate flakes.

Liqueur cheesepots

SERVES 6

450g (1 lb) curd cheese
3 egg yolks
50g (2oz) ground almonds
100g (4oz) demerara sugar
1 tsp vanilla essence
2 tbls Amaretto liqueur
toasted flaked almonds, to decorate

Beat the cheese in a bowl until softened, then beat in the egg yolks, ground almonds, sugar, vanilla essence and liqueur.

Divide the mixture between 6 ramekin dishes and smooth the surface of each. Chill in the refrigerator for 2-3 hours, until firm. Decorate with toasted flaked almonds just before serving.

Mandarin mousse cheesecake

SERVES 8

36 sponge fingers
For the filling
283 g (10 oz) can mandarin oranges,
15 g (½ oz) sachet powdered gelatine
225 g (8 oz) full fat soft cheese
2 eggs, separated
grated rind of 1 orange
100 g (4 oz) caster sugar
142 ml (5 fl oz) carton soured cream
For the topping
142 ml (5 fl oz) carton double cream,
* lightly whipped*
283 g (10 oz) can mandarin oranges,
* drained*

Generously grease a loose-bottomed or spring-form 18-20 cm (7-8 inch) cake tin.

Trim one end from each sponge finger so that it is 7.5 cm (3 inches) long. Line the sides of the greased tin with the sponge fingers, standing them trimmed end down and with the sugared surface against the sides of the tin. Use the remaining sponge fingers and some of the trimmings to line the base of the tin, trimming to fit.

To make the filling, drain the mandarin oranges, reserving 3 tbls of the syrup. Scatter the mandarin oranges over the sponge-finger base.

Pour the reserved mandarin syrup into a small heatproof bowl, sprinkle over the gelatine and leave for 2-3 minutes until spongy. Stand the bowl in a pan of hot water and stir until the gelatine has dissolved. Set aside to cool slightly.

Beat the cheese in a bowl until softened. Beat in the egg yolks, orange rind, half the sugar and the soured cream. Leave the mixture until it is on the point of setting.

Whisk the egg whites until stiff, then whisk in the remaining sugar. Fold lightly into the cheese mixture.

Turn the mixture into the prepared tin and gently tip and tilt it to level the surface. Chill for 3-4 hours, or until set.

Spread the whipped cream over the top of the cheesecake and decorate with mandarin orange segments. Chill for a further 30 minutes.

Run a round-bladed knife around the sides of the cheesecake. Transfer the cheesecake to a serving plate.

Crunchy hazelnut cheesecake

SERVES 8-10

For the base
100 g (4 oz) margarine or butter,
* melted*
225 g (8 oz) digestive biscuits, crushed
For the filling
225 g (8 oz) full fat soft cheese
100 g (4 oz) caster sugar
284 ml (10 fl oz) carton double or
* whipping cream*
2 × 150 g (5.29 oz) cartons hazelnut
* yoghurt*
50 ml (2 oz) roasted, skinned
* hazelnuts*

Grease a loose-bottomed or spring-form 23 cm (9 inch) cake tin.

Mix the melted margarine with the biscuit crumbs. Spoon into the greased tin and press evenly over the base. Chill in the refrigerator while making the filling.

Beat the cheese and sugar in a bowl until smooth. Whip the cream until it forms soft peaks. Fold the cream into the cheese mixture, then fold in the yoghurt.

Turn the mixture into the prepared tin and smooth the surface. Chill in the refrigerator for 3-4 hours, or until set.

Run a round-bladed knife around the sides of the cheesecake, then remove from the tin. Transfer the cheesecake to a serving plate. Arrange the hazelnuts round the edge.

● Top: Mandarin mousse cheesecake; Bottom: Crunchy hazelnut cheesecake

Russian Easter cheesecake

SERVES 8-10

450g (1 lb) curd cheese
75g (3 oz) unsalted butter, softened
a few drops of vanilla essence
1 egg
50g (2 oz) caster sugar
142 ml (5 fl oz) carton soured cream
100g (4 oz) mixed glacé fruit, chopped
50g (2 oz) seedless raisins
50g (2 oz) blanched almonds, toasted
glacé or crystallized fruit, to decorate

Line a spotlessly clean 16cm (6½ inch) diameter, 14.5 cm (5¾ inch) deep clay flower pot with a large piece of scalded muslin or cheesecloth. Make sure that the muslin is pressed well against the base and sides of the pot and allow the excess material to hang down outside the rim. (The excess muslin will be needed to cover the cheese mixture.)

Beat the cheese in a bowl until softened. Add the butter and vanilla essence and beat until the mixture is thoroughly blended.

Whisk the egg and sugar in a mixing bowl until thick and lemon-coloured. Gradually whisk in the cheese mixture, followed by the soured cream. Fold in the fruit and nuts, making sure they are evenly distributed.

Turn the mixture into the lined flower pot. Fold the edges of the muslin neatly over the filling, to cover it. Place a saucer on top and weight down with a 1 kg (2 lb) weight or can. Stand the pot on a wire rack with a large plate underneath to catch the liquid which will drain off as the mixture firms up. Chill in the refrigerator for 24 hours.

To unmould the cheesecake, remove the weight and saucer. Uncover the filling, then invert a serving plate on top of the pot. Hold the plate and pot together and invert. Lift off the pot and carefully remove the muslin.

Smooth the surface of the cheesecake with a round-bladed knife. Decorate with chopped glacé or crystallized fruit.

Serving ideas: This rich, decorative cheesecake is derived from the traditional Russian moulded sweet called Pashka, which is served at Easter accompanied by a light fruited yeast cake. Serve it for a special tea or the dessert course, with slices of sponge cake or sponge biscuit if liked.

Tangy grapefruit cheesecake

SERVES 6

For the base
50g (2 oz) margarine or butter, melted
25g (1 oz) demerara sugar
100g (4 oz) digestive biscuits, crushed
For the filling
15 oz (½ oz) sachet powdered gelatine
3 tbls water
2 × 227g (8 oz) cartons curd cheese
6 tbls fine-cut grapefruit marmalade
2 egg whites
142 ml (5 fl oz) carton double cream, whipped
To decorate
2 grapefruit, peeled and segmented
2-3 tsp caster sugar

Lightly grease a loose-bottomed or spring-form 20 cm (8 inch) cake tin.

Mix the melted margarine with the

sugar and biscuit crumbs. Spoon into the greased tin and press evenly over the base. Chill while making the filling.

Sprinkle the gelatine over the water in a small bowl and leave for 2-3 minutes until spongy. Stand the bowl in a pan of water and stir until the gelatine has dissolved. Leave to cool slightly.

Beat the cheese in a bowl until softened, then gradually beat in the grapefruit marmalade. Stir in the liquid gelatine. Whisk the egg whites until stiff. Fold the cream, then the egg whites into the cheese mixture.

Turn the mixture into the prepared tin and chill for 3-4 hours, until set.

Run a round-bladed knife around the sides of the cheesecake, then remove from the tin. Arrange the drained grapefruit on top. Sprinkle with sugar.

St Clement's cheesecake

SERVES 6

For the base
50 g (2 oz) margarine or butter, melted
25 g (1 oz) demerara sugar
100 g (4 oz) digestive biscuits, crushed
For the filling and decoration
225 g (8 oz) full fat soft cheese
142 ml (5 fl oz) carton double cream
410 g (14½ oz) can condensed milk
2 tsp lemon juice
2 tsp orange juice
crystallized citrus fruit slices

• **Bottom left: Russian Easter cheesecake**
Top left: St Clement's cheesecake
Top right: Tangy grapefruit cheesecake

Mix the melted margarine with the sugar and biscuit crumbs. Spoon into a greased 18 cm (7 inch) flan tin and press evenly over the base and sides. Chill in the refrigerator while making the filling.

Beat the cheese in a bowl until softened, then beat in the cream and milk, followed by the lemon and orange juice. Pour into the prepared flan tin and chill for 2-3 hours or until set, then remove sides of tin.

Decorate the cheesecake with crystallized fruit slices. Serve the cheesecake chilled.

Variations: For Key lime cheesecake, add 1 tsp grated lime rind to the cheese filling and use 4 tsp lime juice instead of the lemon and orange juice. Decorate with lime twists.

For Blackcurrant cheesecake, use blackcurrant cordial instead of lemon and orange juice and top with sugared blackcurrants.

Peach cheesecake

SERVES 8

For the base
18-20 cm (7-8 inch) sponge cake layer,
1 cm (½ inch) thick
For the filling
1½ × 15 g (½ oz) sachets powdered
gelatine
6 tbls water
410 g (14½ oz) can peach slices,
drained
grated rind of ½ orange
2 tbls orange juice
225 g (8 oz) full fat soft cheese
2 eggs, separated
100 g (4 oz) caster sugar
142 ml (5 fl oz) carton soured cream
To decorate
142 ml (5 fl oz) carton double or
whipping cream
410 g (14½ oz) can peach slices,
drained
whole strawberries or redcurrant
sprigs

Lightly grease a loose-bottomed or spring-form 18-20 cm (7-8 inch) cake tin. Place the sponge cake in the greased tin, trimming it if necessary to fit exactly.

To make the filling, sprinkle the gelatine over the water in a heatproof bowl and leave for 2-3 minutes until spongy. Stand the bowl in a pan of hot water and stir until the gelatine has dissolved. Set aside to cool slightly.

Meanwhile, place the peach slices with the orange rind and juice in a blender and blend to a purée.

Beat the cheese in a bowl until softened, then beat in the egg yolks, half the sugar, the soured cream and the peach purée. Stir in the liquid gelatine. Set the mixture aside until it is on the point of setting.

Whisk the egg whites until stiff, then whisk in the remaining sugar. Using a large metal spoon, fold lightly, but thoroughly, into the cheese mixture.

Turn the mixture into the prepared tin and gently tip and tilt it to level the surface. Chill in the refrigerator for 3-4

hours, or until set.

Run a round-bladed knife around the sides of the cheesecake, then remove from the tin. Transfer the cheesecake to a serving plate.

Whip the cream until it forms soft peaks. Pipe or spread the cream over the top of the cheesecake, then decorate with peach slices and strawberries or redcurrants.

Serving ideas: Serve the cheesecake, with a bowl of sugared mixed soft fruit, as part of a summer buffet or for a dinner party dessert.

Bramble cheesecake

SERVES 10-12

For the base
2 medium-size jam-filled Swiss rolls,
cut into 1 cm (½ inch) thick slices
For the filling
2 × 15 g (½ oz) sachets powdered
gelatine
6 tbls water
450 g (1 lb) full fat soft cheese
4 tbls blackberry jelly, melted
225 g (8 oz) caster sugar
4 eggs, separated
284 ml (10 fl oz) carton double or
whipping cream
225 g (8 oz) blackberries
For the topping
284 ml (10 fl oz) carton double or
whipping cream
2 tbls Cointreau
350 g (12 oz) blackberries

Lightly grease a loose-bottomed or spring-form 25-30 cm (10-12 inch) cake tin. Arrange the Swiss roll slices in the base of the tin, pressing them gently together to completely cover the base.

To make the filling, sprinkle the gelatine over the water in a small heatproof bowl and leave for 2-3 minutes until spongy. Stand the bowl in a pan of hot water and stir until the gelatine has dissolved. Set aside to cool slightly.

Beat the cheese in a bowl until softened. Beat in the blackberry jelly, half

• Bramble cheesecake; Peach cheesecake

the sugar, the egg yolks and cream. Stir in the liquid gelatine. Leave the mixture until it is on the point of setting.

Whisk the egg whites until stiff, then whisk in the remaining sugar. Using a large metal spoon, fold lightly, but thoroughly, into the cheese mixture together with the blackberries.

Turn the mixture into the prepared tin and gently tilt and tip it to level the surface. Chill for 3-4 hours, or until set.

Run a round-bladed knife around the sides of the cheesecake, then remove from the tin. Transfer the cheesecake to a serving plate. Whip the cream with the Cointreau until it forms soft peaks, then pipe or swirl over the top. Decorate with blackberries.

Fun-time cheesecake

SERVES 8-10

For the base
50 g (2 oz) margarine or butter, melted
50 g (2 oz) caster sugar
100 g (4 oz) digestive biscuits, crushed
For the filling
15 g (½ oz) sachet powdered gelatine
3 tbls water
227 g (8 oz) carton cottage cheese,
  sieved
2 eggs, separated
100 g (4 oz) caster sugar
grated rind of ½ lemon
a few drops of vanilla essence
150 g (5.29 oz) carton fruit yoghurt
  (any flavour)
assorted small sweets, to decorate

Grease a loose-bottomed or spring-form 18-20 cm (7-8 inch) cake tin.

Mix the melted margarine with the sugar and biscuit crumbs. Spoon into the greased tin and press evenly over the base. Chill in the refrigerator while making the filling.

Sprinkle the gelatine over the water in a small heatproof bowl and leave for 2-3 minutes until spongy. Stand the bowl in a pan of hot water and stir until the gelatine has dissolved. Set aside to cool slightly.

Place the cheese in a mixing bowl and beat in the egg yolks, half the sugar, the lemon rind, vanilla essence and yoghurt. Stir in the liquid gelatine. Leave the mixture until it is on the point of setting.

Whisk the egg whites until stiff, then whisk in the remaining sugar. Using a large metal spoon, fold lightly, but thoroughly, into the cheese mixture.

Turn the mixture into the prepared tin and gently tip and tilt it to level the surface. Chill for 3-4 hours, or until set.

Run a round-bladed knife around the sides of the cheesecake, then remove from the tin. Transfer the cheesecake to a plate. Decorate with sweets.

Gooseberry fool cheesecake

SERVES 6

For the filling
450 g (1 lb) fresh gooseberries, thawed
  and drained if frozen
75 g (3 oz) sugar
15 g (½ oz) sachet powdered gelatine
3 tbls water
225 g (8 oz) full fat soft cheese
142 ml (5 fl oz) carton double cream,
  whipped
To decorate
100 g (4 oz) gingernut biscuits,
  crushed
whole dessert gooseberries

Lightly grease a loose-bottomed or spring-form 18 cm (7 inch) cake tin.

Place the gooseberries and sugar in a saucepan, cover and stew gently until soft, then sieve into a bowl.

Sprinkle the gelatine over the water in a small heatproof bowl and leave for 2-3 minutes until spongy. Stand the bowl in a pan of hot water and stir until the gelatine has dissolved, then stir into the gooseberry purée. Set aside to cool slightly.

Beat the cheese in a bowl until softened, then fold in the cream and gooseberry purée. Turn the mixture into the greased tin and chill in the refrigerator for 3-4 hours, or until set.

Run a round-bladed knife around the sides of the cheesecake, then remove from the tin. Transfer the cheesecake to a serving plate and decorate with crushed biscuits and whole gooseberries.

Variations: Tint the gooseberry cheese mixture pale green with a little food colouring, if liked.

For a Rhubarb Cheesecake, use rhubarb instead of gooseberries in the filling and tint lightly with cochineal. Top with orange segments.

• Top: Gooseberry fool cheesecake; Bottom: Fun-time cheesecake

Prawn cocktail cheesecake

SERVES 8-10

For the base
100g (4oz) margarine or butter,
   melted
175g (6oz) water biscuits, crushed
3 tbls chopped fresh parsley
salt and pepper
For the filling
2 × 15g (½oz) sachets powdered
   gelatine
6 tbls water
450g (1 lb) full fat soft cheese
grated rind of 1 lemon
2 tbls lemon juice
4 eggs, separated
1 tbls tomato purée
284 ml (10 fl oz) carton soured cream
175g (6oz) prawns, thawed if frozen,
   chopped
To finish
175g (6oz) full fat soft cheese
3 tbls thick mayonnaise
4 tbls chopped fresh parsley
juice of ½ lemon
8 whole prawns, to garnish

Grease a loose-bottomed or spring-form 25-30 cm (10-12 inch) cake tin.

Mix the melted margarine with the biscuit crumbs and parsley. Season to taste. Spoon the mixture into the greased tin and press evenly over the base. Chill in the refrigerator while making the filling.

Sprinkle the gelatine over the water in a small heatproof bowl and leave for 2-3 minutes until spongy. Stand the bowl in a pan of hot water and leave until the gelatine has dissolved. Set aside to cool slightly.

Beat the cheese in a bowl until softened. Beat in the lemon rind and juice, egg yolks, tomato purée and soured cream. Stir in the liquid gelatine and season to taste. Leave the mixture until on the point of setting.

Whisk the egg whites until stiff. Using a large metal spoon, fold lightly, but thoroughly, into the cheese mixture with the chopped prawns. Turn the mixture into the prepared tin and gently tilt and tip it to level the surface. Chill the cheesecake in the refrigerator for 3-4 hours, or until set.

Run a round-bladed knife around the sides of the cheesecake, then remove the cheesecake from the tin and transfer to a serving plate.

Beat the cheese with the mayonnaise, parsley and lemon juice until very smooth. Pipe or spread the cheese over the top of the cheesecake. Garnish with prawns.

Neapolitan cheesecake

SERVES 6-8

For the base
75g (3oz) margarine or butter, melted
175g (6oz) digestive biscuits, crushed
25g (1oz) grated Parmesan cheese
salt and pepper
For the filling
15g (½oz) sachet powdered gelatine
3 tbls water
225g (8oz) full fat soft cheese
1 tbls tomato purée
½ tsp caster sugar
2 eggs, separated
1 small onion, grated
142 ml (5 fl oz) carton double or
   whipping cream
1 tbls chopped fresh basil
4 large tomatoes, skinned, seeded
   and chopped
To garnish
small tomatoes, sliced or quartered
fresh basil leaves

● Prawn cocktail cheesecake; Neapolitan cheesecake

Grease a loose-bottomed or spring-form 18-20 cm (7-8 inch) cake tin.

Mix the melted margarine with the biscuit crumbs and grated cheese and season to taste. Spoon into the greased tin and press evenly over the base. Chill in the refrigerator while making the filling.

Sprinkle the gelatine over the water in a small heatproof bowl and leave for 2-3 minutes until spongy. Stand the bowl in a pan of hot water and stir until the gelatine has dissolved. Set aside to cool slightly.

Beat the cheese in a bowl until softened. Beat in the tomato purée, sugar, egg yolks, onion, cream and basil. Stir in the liquid gelatine and season to

taste. Leave the mixture until it is on the point of setting.

Whisk the egg whites until stiff. Using a large metal spoon, fold lightly, but thoroughly, into the cheese mixture with the chopped tomatoes. Turn the mixture into the prepared tin and gently tilt and tip it to level the surface. Chill for 3-4 hours, or until set.

Run a round-bladed knife around the sides of the cheesecake, then remove from the tin. Transfer to a plate and garnish with tomatoes and basil.

Variation: For Egg and tomato cheesecake, replace half the chopped tomatoes in the filling with 2 chopped hard-boiled eggs.

49

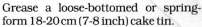

Cool cucumber cheesecake

SERVES 6-8

For the base
75 g (3 oz) margarine or butter, melted
175 g (6 oz) water biscuits, crushed
grated rind of ½ lemon
1 tbls lemon juice
salt and pepper
For the filling
½ large cucumber, coarsely grated
15 g (½ oz) sachet powdered gelatine
3 tbls water
225 g (8 oz) full fat soft cheese
2 eggs, separated
grated rind of ½ lemon
1 tbls chopped fresh mint or 1 tsp dried mint
142 ml (5 fl oz) carton soured cream
1 garlic clove, crushed
For the garnish
cucumber slices
fresh mint sprigs

Grease a loose-bottomed or spring-form 18-20 cm (7-8 inch) cake tin.

Thoroughly mix together the base ingredients. Spoon into the greased tin and press evenly over the base. Chill while making the filling.

Wrap the grated cucumber in a piece of muslin or clean thin cloth and squeeze to drain thoroughly.

Sprinkle the gelatine over the water in a small heatproof bowl and leave for 2-3 minutes until spongy. Stand the bowl in a pan of hot water and stir until the mixture has dissolved. Set aside to cool slightly.

Beat the cheese in a bowl. Beat in the egg yolks, lemon rind, mint, soured cream and garlic. Stir in the gelatine and cucumber and season to taste. Leave until on the point of setting.

Whisk the egg whites until stiff. Fold into the cheese mixture.

Turn the mixture into the prepared tin and gently tilt and tip it to level the surface. Chill for 3-4 hours, until set.

Run a round-bladed knife around sides of the cheesecake. Transfer to a plate. Garnish with cucumber slices and mint sprigs.

Cheesecake florentine

SERVES 6-8

For the base
75 g (3 oz) margarine or butter, melted
175 g (6 oz) water biscuits, crushed
salt and pepper
For the filling
275 g (10 oz) full fat soft cheese
3 eggs, separated
50 g (2 oz) Cheddar cheese, grated
grated rind of 1 lemon
25 g (1 oz) plain flour, sifted
pinch of grated nutmeg
142 ml (5 fl oz) carton soured cream
225 g (8 oz) packet frozen chopped spinach, thawed and thoroughly drained
For the topping
142 ml (5 fl oz) carton soured cream
2 hard-boiled eggs, sliced
chopped fresh parsley

Heat the oven to 160°C, 325°F, Gas Mark 3. Grease a loose-bottomed or spring-form 18-20 cm (7-8 inch) cake tin.

Mix the melted margarine with the biscuit crumbs and season to taste. Spoon the mixture into the greased tin and press evenly over the base. Chill in the refrigerator while making the filling.

Beat the full fat cheese in a bowl until softened. Beat in the egg yolks, grated cheese, lemon rind, flour, nutmeg, and soured cream. Season to taste, then stir in the spinach.

Whisk the egg whites until stiff. Using a large metal spoon, fold lightly, but thoroughly, into the cheese mixture. Turn the mixture into the prepared tin and smooth the surface. Place the cheesecake on a baking sheet and bake in the oven for 1½-1¾ hours, or until the filling is set.

● Bottom left: Cool cucumber cheesecake
Top: Cheesecake florentine

Just before the cheesecake is cooked, gently warm through the soured cream for the topping in a saucepan without allowing to boil.

Remove the cheesecake from the oven. Run a round-bladed knife around the sides of the cheesecake, then remove from the tin. Transfer the cheesecake to a warmed serving plate. Arrange the egg slices on top, then spoon over the soured cream and scatter with chopped parsley.

Variation: For the topping, use tomato slices instead of egg, and sprinkle with finely chopped fresh basil or marjoram instead of parsley.

Mariner's cheesecake

SERVE 6-8

For the base
100g (4 oz) plain flour
pinch of salt
25g (1 oz) margarine or butter, diced
25g (1 oz) lard, diced
4 tsp cold water
For the filling
225g (8 oz) smoked haddock fillet
150 ml (¼ pint) milk
4 tsp lemon juice
275g (10 oz) curd or sieved cottage
    cheese
3 eggs, separated
pinch of grated nutmeg
grated rind of 1 lemon
25g (1 oz) plain flour, sifted
142 ml (5 fl oz) carton soured cream
salt and pepper
For the topping
3 tbls soured cream
2 hard-boiled eggs
2 tbls chopped fresh parsley

Lightly grease a loose-bottomed or spring-form 18-20 cm (7-8 inch) cake tin.

Sift the flour with the salt into a mixing bowl. Add the margarine and lard and rub into the flour with the fingertips until the mixture resembles fine breadcrumbs. Sprinkle over the water and mix it in with a round-bladed knife. Draw the mixture together to make a firm dough, adding a few drops more water if it feels too dry.

Turn the dough on to a lightly floured surface and knead gently for 1 minute until smooth.

Roll out the dough on a lightly floured surface and use to line the base of the greased tin. Chill in the refrigerator while making the filling.

Heat the oven to 160°C, 325°F, Gas Mark 3.

To make the filling, put the haddock into a shallow pan with the milk and lemon juice. Cover and simmer very gently until the fish is opaque and flakes easily. Drain the fish, remove

• Left: Pizza cheesecake; Right: Mariner's cheesecake

and discard the skin, then flake the flesh finely with a fork.

Beat the cheese in a bowl until softened. Beat in the egg yolks, nutmeg, lemon rind, flour and soured cream. Stir in the flaked haddock and season to taste.

Whisk the egg whites until stiff. Using a large metal spoon, fold lightly, but thoroughly, into the cheese mixture. Turn the mixture into the prepared tin and smooth the surface. Bake in the oven for 1½-1¾ hours, until the filling is set.

Spread the soured cream for the topping over the top of the cheesecake and return to the oven for 3-5 minutes. Meanwhile, finely chop the eggs and mix well with the parsley.

Remove the cheesecake from the oven. Run a round-bladed knife around the sides of the cheesecake, then remove the sides of the tin. Transfer the cheesecake to a heated serving plate and sprinkle with the egg and parsley mixture. Serve immediately.

Pizza cheesecake

For the base
100 g (4 oz) plain flour
pinch of salt
25 g (1 oz) lard
4 tbls water
For the filling
1½ tbls olive oil
50 g (2 oz) button mushrooms, sliced
1 tbls plain flour
75 ml (3½ fl oz) milk
½ tsp tomato purée
50 g (2 oz) Cheddar cheese, grated
salt and pepper
113 g (4 oz) carton curd or sieved
*   cottage cheese*
1 egg, separated
1 egg yolk
For the topping
75 g (3 oz) Mozzarella cheese, cut into
*   strips*
8 black olives
tomato slices, halved
1 tbls chopped mixed fresh herbs
1-2 tsp olive oil

Heat the oven to 160°C, 325°F, Gas Mark 3. Lightly oil an 18-20 cm (7-8 inch) flan ring on a baking sheet.

Sift the flour with the salt into a mixing bowl. Put the lard into a saucepan with the water and stir over low heat until melted. Pour on to the flour and mix to a soft dough. Roll out the dough on a lightly floured surface and use to line the greased flan ring. Chill in the refrigerator while making the filling.

To make the filling, heat the oil in a saucepan, add the mushrooms and cook for 5-6 minutes or until just tender. Remove the mushrooms with a slotted spoon and reserve.

Stir the flour into the oil remaining in the pan and cook, stirring, for 1 minute. Gradually stir in the milk. Bring slowly to the boil and simmer, stirring, until the sauce has thickened. Remove from the heat and stir in the tomato purée and grated cheese, and season.

Beat the curd cheese in a bowl until softened. Beat in the cheese sauce and egg yolks. Whisk the egg white until stiff. Using a large metal spoon, fold lightly, but thoroughly, into the cheese mixture, together with the cooked mushrooms.

Turn the mixture into the prepared flan ring and smooth the surface. Bake in the oven for 1½ hours, or until set.

Remove the cheesecake from the oven. Increase the oven heat to 230°C, 450°F, Gas Mark 8.

Arrange the Mozzarella slices in a lattice pattern over the top of the cheesecake. Add the olives and tomatoes and sprinkle over the herbs. Season to taste, then drizzle over the oil. Return the cheesecake to the oven for about 10 minutes, or until the Mozzarella has melted.

Remove the cheesecake from the oven. Run a round-bladed knife around the sides of the cheesecake, then remove from the ring. Transfer to a serving plate. Serve immediately.

Variations: Ring the changes by adding slices of salami, fried mushrooms, thinly sliced red or green pepper or anchovy fillets to the topping.

Mushroom cheesecake

SERVES 6-8

For the base
100g (4 oz) plain flour
pinch of salt
25g (1 oz) lard
4 tbls water
For the filling
40g (1½oz) margarine or butter
100g (4 oz) button mushrooms, sliced
2 tbls plain flour
75 ml (3 fl oz) milk
½ tsp French mustard
50g (2 oz) mature Cheddar cheese,
* grated*
salt and pepper
113g (4 oz) carton curd or sieved
* cottage cheese*
1 egg, separated
1 egg yolk
For the topping
25g (1 oz) margarine or butter
50g (2 oz) button mushrooms, sliced
50g (2 oz) mature Cheddar cheese,
* grated*
a little paprika (optional)

Heat the oven to 160°C, 325°F, Gas
Mark 3. Grease an 18-20 cm (7-8 inch)
flan ring on a baking sheet.

Sift the flour with the salt into a mixing bowl. Put the lard into a saucepan
with the water and stir over low heat
until melted. Pour on to the flour and
mix to a soft dough. Roll out on a lightly
floured surface and use to line the
greased flan ring. Chill in the refrigerator while making the filling.

To make the filling, melt the margarine in a saucepan, add the mushrooms
and cook for 5-6 minutes or until just
tender. Remove the mushrooms with a
slotted spoon and reserve.

Stir the flour into the fat remaining
in the pan and cook, stirring, for 1
minute. Gradually stir in the milk,
bring slowly to the boil and cook, stirring, until the sauce has thickened.
Remove from heat. Beat in the mustard
and grated cheese. Season to taste.

Beat the curd cheese in a bowl until
softened. Beat in the cheese sauce and

egg yolks. Whisk the egg white until
stiff. Fold into the cheese mixture with
the cooked mushrooms.

Turn the mixture into the prepared
flan ring and smooth the surface. Bake
in the oven for 35-40 minutes, or until set.

Just before the cheesecake is cooked,
prepare the topping. Melt the margarine in a frying pan, add the mushrooms
and fry gently until just tender. Drain
the mushrooms on absorbent paper,
then arrange on top of the cheesecake.
Sprinkle over the grated cheese. Return to the oven for a further 15 minutes, until the topping is melted.

Remove the cheesecake from the
oven. Run a round-bladed knife
around the sides of the cheesecake,
then remove from the ring. Transfer
the cheesecake to a warmed serving
plate and dust lightly with paprika, if
using. Serve immediately.

Stilton cheesecake

SERVES 10-12

For the base
100g (4 oz) margarine or butter,
* melted*
175g (6 oz) water biscuits, crushed
2 tbls poppy seeds
garlic salt
black pepper
For the filling
2 × 15g (½oz) sachets powdered
* gelatine*
6 tbls water
300g (11 oz) full fat soft cheese
175g (6 oz) Stilton cheese, crumbled
4 eggs, separated
1 tsp French mustard
284 ml (10 fl oz) carton double or
* whipping cream*
garlic salt
black pepper
100g (4 oz) walnuts, chopped
To garnish
16 walnut halves
celery leaves
90g (3½oz) full fat soft cheese
a little paprika (optional)

Grease a loose-bottomed or spring-form 25-30 cm (10-12 inch) cake tin.

Mix the melted margarine with the biscuit crumbs and poppy seeds. Season to taste with garlic salt and pepper. Spoon into tin and press evenly over base. Chill while making filling.

Sprinkle the gelatine over the water in a small heatproof bowl and leave for 2-3 minutes until spongy. Stand the bowl in a pan of hot water and stir until dissolved. Leave to cool slightly.

Beat the full fat cheese in a bowl until softened, add the Stilton and beat until thoroughly blended. Beat in the egg yolks, mustard, cream and liquid gelatine. Season with garlic salt and pep-

per. Leave until on the point of setting.

Whisk the egg whites until stiff. Using a large metal spoon, fold into the cheese mixture with the chopped walnuts. Turn the mixture into the tin and gently tilt and tip it to level the surface. Chill for 3-4 hours, until set.

Run a round-bladed knife around the sides of the cheesecake to loosen it, then remove from the tin. Transfer the cheesecake to a serving plate. For the garnish arrange the walnut halves and celery leaves on top of the cheesecake. Beat the cheese until soft and creamy, then place in a piping bag and pipe dots of cheese around the edge of the cheesecake. Dust lightly with paprika, if using.

● Top: Mushroom cheesecake; Bottom: Stilton cheesecake

Creamy broccoli cheesecake

SERVES 6-8

For the base
100 g (4 oz) plain flour
salt
25 g (1 oz) margarine or butter, diced
25 g (1 oz) lard, diced
4 tsp cold water
For the filling
225 g (8 oz) broccoli spears
275 g (10 oz) curd cheese or sieved
   cottage cheese
3 eggs, separated
grated rind of ½ lemon
3 tbls chopped fresh parsley
25 g (1 oz) plain flour, sifted
6 tbls soured cream
To garnish
142 ml (5 fl oz) carton soured cream
black pepper
blanched broccoli florets

Sift the flour with a pinch of salt into a mixing bowl. Add the margarine and lard and rub in with the fingertips until the mixture resembles fine breadcrumbs. Sprinkle over the water and mix it in with a round-bladed knife. Draw the mixture together to make a firm dough, adding a few drops more water if it feels too dry.

Turn the dough on to a lightly floured surface and knead gently for 1 minute until smooth.

Lightly grease a loose-bottomed or spring-form 18-20 cm (7-8 inch) cake tin. Roll out the pastry on a lightly floured surface and use to line the base of the tin. Chill in the refrigerator while making the filling.

Heat the oven to 200°C, 400°F, Gas Mark 6.

To make the filling, cook the broccoli in a saucepan of boiling, salted water until tender. Thoroughly drain the broccoli, then chop roughly.

Prick the pastry base all over with a fork, then bake in the oven for 10-15 minutes, until golden. Remove from the oven and allow to cool.

Beat the cheese in a bowl until sof-

tened. Beat in the egg yolks, lemon rind, parsley, the flour, and the 6 tbls soured cream. Beat in the chopped broccoli, then season to taste.

Whisk the egg whites until stiff. Using a large metal spoon, fold lightly, but thoroughly, into the cheese mixture. Turn the mixture into the prepared tin and smooth the surface.

Bake in the oven for 1½-1¾ hours or until the filling is set.

Remove the cheesecake from the oven. Run a round-bladed knife around the side of the cheesecake, then remove the sides of the tin. Transfer the cheesecake to a plate and leave to cool completely.

Whisk the soured cream with a fork and season with pepper, then spread over the cheesecake. Garnish with broccoli florets.

Festive turkey cheesecake

SERVES 6-8

For the base
75 g (3 oz) margarine or butter, melted
100 g (4 oz) water biscuits, crushed
4 tbls dry packet sage and onion
   stuffing mix
For the filling
275 g (10 oz) curd or sieved cottage
   cheese
3 eggs, separated
25 g (1 oz) plain flour, sifted
175 g (6 oz) cooked turkey meat, finely
   chopped or minced
2 tbls chopped fresh parsley
142 ml (5 fl oz) carton soured cream
salt and pepper
For the topping
25 g (1 oz) margarine or butter
1 medium onion, thinly sliced
142 ml (5 fl oz) carton soured cream
fried onion rings
a little cranberry sauce

Heat the oven to 160°C, 325°F, Gas Mark 3. Thoroughly grease a loose-bottomed or spring-form 18-20 cm (7-8 inch) cake tin.

● Festive turkey cheesecake: Creamy broccoli cheesecake

Mix the melted margarine with the biscuit crumbs and stuffing mix. Spoon into the greased tin and press evenly over the base.

To make the filling, beat the cheese in a bowl until softened. Beat in the egg yolks, flour, turkey, parsley and soured cream. Season to taste. Whisk the egg whites until stiff and fold lightly, but thoroughly, into the cheese mixture.

Turn the mixture into the tin and level the surface. Place the cheesecake on a baking sheet and bake in the oven for 1½-1¾ hours, or until set.

Just before the cheesecake is cooked,

make the topping. Melt the margarine in a frying pan, add the onion and fry gently until golden. Add the soured cream and stir until well mixed and heated through, but do not allow to boil. Remove from heat and keep warm.

Remove the cheesecake from the oven. Run a round-bladed knife around the sides of the cheesecake, then remove from the tin. Transfer the cheesecake to a warmed serving plate. Spread the onion mixture over the top of the cheesecake, garnish with onion rings and spoon a little cranberry sauce into the centre. Serve immediately.

Herby avocado cheesecake

SERVES 6-8

For the base
75 g (3 oz) margarine or butter, melted
175 g (6 oz) Melba toast, crushed
grated rind of ½ lemon
salt and pepper
For the filling
15 g (½ oz) sachet powdered gelatine
3 tbls water
1 large avocado, halved and stoned
grated rind of ½ lemon
1 tbls lemon juice
225 g (8 oz) herb-flavoured full fat soft
    cheese
2 eggs, separated
142 ml (5 fl oz) carton soured cream
To garnish
1 avocado, sliced
2 tbls lemon juice
parsley sprigs

Grease a loose-bottomed or spring-form 18-20 cm (7-8 inch) cake tin.

Mix the melted margarine with the toast crumbs and lemon rind and season to taste. Spoon into the greased tin and press evenly over the base. Chill in the refrigerator while making the avocado filling.

Sprinkle the gelatine over the water in a small heatproof bowl and leave for 2-3 minutes until spongy. Stand the bowl in a pan of hot water and stir until the gelatine has dissolved. Set aside to cool slightly.

Scoop the avocado flesh into a bowl and mash with lemon rind and juice until smooth.

Beat the cheese in a separate bowl until softened. Beat in the egg yolks, soured cream and avocado purée. Stir in the liquid gelatine and season to taste. Leave the mixture until it is on the point of setting.

Whisk the egg whites until stiff. Using a large metal spoon, fold lightly, but thoroughly, into the cheese mixture. Turn the mixture into the prepared tin and gently tilt and tip it to level the surface. Chill the cheesecake

in the refrigerator for 3-4 hours, or until set.

Run a round-bladed knife around the sides of the cheesecake, then remove from the tin. Transfer the cheesecake to a serving plate. To garnish, turn the avocado slices in the lemon juice to prevent them from discolouring. Arrange the avocado slices and parsley sprigs on top of the cheesecake.

Serving ideas: Serve as a starter or light main course, with Melba toast or crisp crackers and a dry or medium white wine.

Ham and onion cheesecake

SERVES 6-8

For the base
100 g (4 oz) plain flour
pinch of salt
25 g (1 oz) lard
4 tbls water
For the filling
300 g (11 oz) curd or sieved cottage
    cheese
3 eggs, separated
25 g (1 oz) plain flour, sifted
1 small onion, grated
100 g (4 oz) cooked ham, chopped
142 ml (5 fl oz) carton double or
    whipping cream
For the topping
2 tomatoes, sliced
50 g (2 oz) Double Gloucester cheese,
    grated

Heat the oven to 160°C, 325°F, Gas Mark 3. Grease a loose-bottomed or spring-form 18-20 cm (7-8 inch) cake tin.

Sift the flour with the salt into a mixing bowl. Put the lard into a saucepan with the water and stir over low heat until melted. Pour on to the flour and mix to a soft dough.

Press the dough evenly over the base of the greased tin and about 2.5 cm (1 inch) of the way up the sides. Chill while making the filling.

To make the filling, beat the cheese in a bowl until softened. Beat in the egg yolks, flour, onion, ham and cream. Season to taste.

Whisk the egg whites until stiff. Using a large metal spoon, fold lightly, but thoroughly, into the cheese mixture. Spoon the mixture into the prepared tin and smooth the surface. Bake the cheesecake in the oven for 1½

hours, or until the filling is set firm.

Arrange the tomato slices on top of the cheesecake, then sprinkle over the cheese. Return the cheesecake to the oven for a further 15 minutes, until the cheese topping is melted, and golden.

Remove from the oven. Run a round-bladed knife around the sides of the cheesecake, then carefully remove from the tin. Transfer the cheesecake to a warmed serving plate and serve.

● Top: Ham and onion cheesecake; Below: Herby avocado cheesecake

Crispy potato cheesecake

SERVES 4-6

For the base
100 g (4 oz) plain flour
pinch of salt
25 g (1 oz) lard
4 tbls water
For the filling
2 medium potatoes, coarsely grated
salt
113 g (4 oz) carton curd or sieved
  cottage cheese
1 egg, separated
1 egg yolk
2 tbls plain flour, sifted
25 g (1 oz) grated Parmesan cheese
65 ml (2½ fl oz) milk
3 spring onions, finely chopped
For the topping
142 ml (5 fl oz) carton soured cream
potato crisps

Heat the oven to 160°C, 325°F, Gas Mark 3. Lightly grease an 18-20 cm (7-8 inch) flan ring on a baking sheet.

Sift the flour with the salt into a mix-ing bowl. Put the lard into a saucepan with the water and stir over low heat until melted. Pour on to the flour and mix to a soft dough. Roll out and use to line the greased tin. Chill in the re-frigerator while making the filling.

To make the filling, place the grated potatoes in a bowl of salted water until required. Beat the curd cheese in a bowl until softened. Beat in the egg yolks, flour, grated cheese, milk and onions.

Drain the potatoes, wrap in a piece of muslin or clean thin cloth and squeeze out as much moisture as possible, then stir into the cheese mixture. Season to taste. Whisk the egg white until stiff. Fold lightly, but thoroughly, into the cheese mixture.

Pour the mixture into the prepared tin and smooth the surface. Bake in the oven for 40-50 minutes, or until set.

Just before the cheesecake is cooked, gently warm the soured cream in a small saucepan, but do not boil.

Remove the cheesecake from the oven. Run a round-bladed knife around the sides of the cheesecake, then remove from the ring. Transfer the cheesecake to a heated serving plate. Top with the soured cream and crisps. Serve immediately.

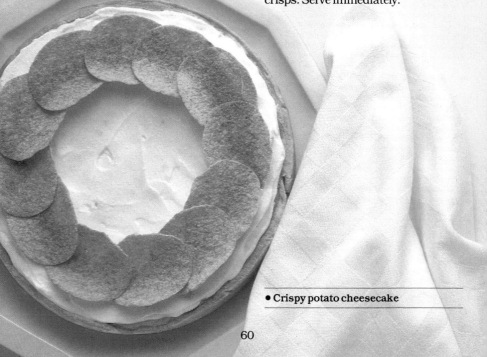

● Crispy potato cheesecake

Tuna cheesecake

SERVES 6-8

For the base
75 g (3 oz) margarine or butter, melted
175 g (6 oz) water biscuits, crushed
salt and pepper

For the filling
15 g (½ oz) sachet powdered gelatine
3 tbls water
225 g (8 oz) full fat soft cheese
2 eggs, separated
grated rind of ½ lemon
4 tsp lemon juice
198 g (7 oz) can tuna, drained
142 ml (5 fl oz) carton soured cream
2 hard-boiled eggs, finely chopped
stuffed olives, to garnish

Grease a loose-bottomed or spring-form 18-20 cm (7-8 inch) cake tin.

Mix the melted margarine with the biscuit crumbs. Season to taste. Spoon into the greased tin and press evenly over the base. Chill while making the filling.

Sprinkle the gelatine over the water in a small heatproof bowl and leave for 2-3 minutes until spongy. Stand the bowl in a pan of hot water and stir until dissolved. Set aside to cool slightly.

Beat the cheese in a bowl until softened. Beat in the egg yolks, lemon rind and juice, tuna, soured cream and hard-boiled eggs. Stir in gelatine and season. Leave until about to set.

Whisk the egg whites until stiff. Using a large metal spoon, fold lightly, but thoroughly, into the cheese mixture. Turn into prepared tin and smooth surface. Chill for 3-4 hours, or until set.

Run a round-bladed knife around the sides of the cheesecake, then remove from the tin. Transfer the cheesecake to a plate. Garnish with olives.

Summer salad cheesecake

SERVES 8-10

For the base
100g (4 oz) margarine, melted
175g (6 oz) water biscuits, crushed
50g (2 oz) grated Parmesan cheese
salt and pepper
For the filling
2 × 15g (½ oz) sachets powdered gelatine
6 tbls water
450g (1 lb) full fat soft cheese
4 eggs, separated
75g (3 oz) grated Parmesan cheese
142 ml (5 fl oz) carton double cream
150 ml (¼ pint) thick mayonnaise
1 large red pepper, chopped
½ small cucumber, thinly sliced
100g (4 oz) cooked ham, diced
rings of red pepper, to garnish

Grease a loose-bottomed or spring-form 20 cm (8 inch) cake tin.

Mix the melted margarine with the biscuit crumbs and grated cheese and season to taste. Spoon into the greased tin and press evenly over the base. Chill while making the filling.

Sprinkle the gelatine over the water in a small heatproof bowl and leave for 2-3 minutes until spongy. Stand the bowl in a pan of hot water and stir until dissolved. Leave to cool slightly.

Beat the soft cheese in a bowl. Beat in the egg yolks, grated cheese, cream and mayonnaise. Stir in the gelatine and season. Leave until about to set.

Whisk the egg whites until stiff. Fold into the cheese mixture. Spoon one-half of the mixture into the tin and smooth surface. Scatter the red pepper, cucumber and ham over the top. Cover with the remaining cheese mixture and smooth surface. Chill for 3-4 hours, until set.

Run a round-bladed knife around sides of cheesecake. Transfer to a plate. Garnish with pepper rings.

Watercress cheesecake

SERVES 6-8

For the base
75g (3 oz) margarine or butter, melted
175g (6 oz) oatcakes, crushed
salt and pepper
For the filling
15g (½ oz) sachet powdered gelatine
3 tbls water
225g (8 oz) full fat soft cheese
2 eggs, separated
50g (2 oz) watercress, finely chopped
4 spring onions, finely chopped
284 ml (10 fl oz) carton soured cream
watercress sprigs, to garnish

Grease a loose-bottomed or spring-form 18-20 cm (7-8 inch) cake tin. Mix the melted margarine with the oatcake crumbs and season to taste. Spoon into the greased tin and press evenly over the base. Chill in the refrigerator while making the filling.

Sprinkle the gelatine over the water in a small heatproof bowl and leave for 2-3 minutes until spongy. Stand the bowl in a pan of hot water and stir until the gelatine has dissolved. Set aside to cool slightly.

Beat the cheese in a bowl until softened. Beat in the egg yolks, chopped watercress, spring onions and half the soured cream. Stir in the liquid gelatine and season to taste. Leave the mixture until it is on the point of setting.

Whisk the egg whites until stiff. Using a large metal spoon, fold lightly, but thoroughly, into the cheese mixture. Turn into the tin and gently tilt and tip it to level the surface. Chill the cheesecake in the refrigerator for 3-4 hours, or until set.

Run a round-bladed knife around the sides of the cheesecake, then remove from the tin. Transfer the cheesecake to a serving plate. Spread the remaining soured cream over the top, then garnish with watercress sprigs.

• Top: Summer salad cheesecake; Bottom: Watercress cheesecake

INDEX

Note: this index includes variations suggested in recipes as well as the main recipes.